Do you believe that cynicism is simply common sense?

Do sunny smiles make you want to snarl? Do you have the feeling you may answer with something unprintable the next time you hear "Have a nice day"? Then you'll be in the best of company with the whiplash wits and sardonic savants brought together in *The Portable Curmudgeon*. From Aristotle to Frank Zappa, from Tallulah Bankhead to Oscar Wilde, from Woody Allen to Leo Tolstoy, the quotations on these pages run like rapiers through the entire alphabet of annoyances. In addition to this wealth of wickedly barbed wit and wisdom, there are full-length profiles of and interviews with the towering world-class curmudgeons of past and present. Ideal for browsing, conveniently arranged A to Z for instant reference to the pet peeve of your choice, here is *the* essential companion to all who agree with W. C. Field's immortal credo: "I am free of all prejudices. I hate everyone equally."

JON WINOKUR has compiled and edited many books, including *The Portable Curmudgeon Redux, A Curmudgeon's Garden of Love, Zen to Go, Friendly Advice, Mondo Canine,* and *True Confessions.* He has been in a bad mood since 1963.

cur·mud·geon \ˌkər-ˈməj-ən *n* [origin unknown]
1 *archaic*: a crusty, ill-tempered, churlish old man
2 *modern*: anyone who hates hypocrisy and pretense and has the temerity to say so; anyone with the habit of pointing out unpleasant facts in an engaging and humorous manner

THE
P·O·R·T·A·B·L·E
CURMUDGEON

COMPILED AND EDITED BY
JON WINOKUR

A PLUME BOOK

PLUME
Published by the Penguin Group
Penguin Books USA Inc., 375 Hudson Street, New York, New York 10014, U.S.A.
Penguin Books Ltd, 27 Wrights Lane, London W8 5TZ, England
Penguin Books Australia Ltd, Ringwood, Victoria, Australia
Penguin Books Canada Ltd, 10 Alcorn Avenue, Toronto, Ontario, Canada M4V 3B2
Penguin Books (N.Z.) Ltd, 182-190 Wairau Road, Auckland 10, New Zealand

Penguin Books Ltd, Registered Offices: Harmondsworth, Middlesex, England

Published by Plume, an imprint of New American Library, a division of Penguin Books USA Inc.
Previously published in an NAL Books edition.

First Plume Printing, October, 1992
20

ACKNOWLEDGMENTS
The author acknowledges Carcanet Press Ltd. for permission to include extracts from *Half-Truths and One-and-a-Half Truths: Selected Aphorisms of Karl Kraus,* edited and translated by Harry Zohn, copyright © 1976, 1986, by Harry Zohn.

 REGISTERED TRADEMARK—MARCA REGISTRADA

LIBRARY OF CONGRESS CATALOGING-IN-PUBLICATION DATA
The Portable curmudgeon / compiled and edited by Jon Winokur.
       p.   cm.
    ISBN 0-452-26668-8
    1. Quotations. English.   2. American wit and humor.   I. Winokur, Jon.
[PN6083.P48   1992b]
081—dc20   92-53550
                                                                       CIP
Printed in the United States of America
Original hardcover design by Barbara Huntley

TO NOBODY

ACKNOWLEDGMENTS

The following well-meaning persons insisted on trying to help: Peter Bell, Reid Boates, Norrie Epstein, Ron Hammes, Nancy Lea Johnson, Howard LeNoble, Anita Nelson, Susan Nethery, John Paine, Al Rasof, Susan Rogers, Tobi Sanders, Steve Schuhle, Susan Soriano, Nancy Steele, Linda Takahashi, Lawrence Teacher, Stuart Teacher, LuAnn Walther, Robert Weide of Whyaduck Productions, Elinor Winokur, and Mark Wolgin.

CONTENTS

It is a fine thing to face machine guns for immortality and a medal, but isn't it a fine thing, too, to face calumny, injustice and loneliness for the truth which makes men free?
—H. L. MENCKEN

THE PORTABLE CURMUDGEON

INTRODUCTION

Dictionaries define *curmudgeon* as a churlish, irascible fellow; a cantankerous old codger. The origin of the word is unknown, but it might come from an old Scottish word that meant "murmur" or "mumble," or from the French *coeur mechant*, "evil heart." The archaic definition made it a synonym for *miser*, and the word has had recent currency in a somewhat milder connotation, to describe a not entirely unlikable grouch.

A curmudgeon's reputation for malevolence is undeserved. They're neither warped nor evil at heart. They don't hate mankind, just mankind's excesses. They're just as sensitive and soft-hearted as the next guy, but they hide their vulnerability beneath a crust of misanthropy. They ease the pain by turning hurt into humor. They snarl at pretense and bite at hypocrisy out of a healthy sense of outrage. They attack maudlinism because it devalues genuine sentiment. They hurl polemical thunderbolts at middle-class values and pop culture in order to preserve their sanity. Nature, having failed to equip them with a serviceable denial mechanism, has endowed them with astute perception and sly wit. Offense is their only defense. Their weapons are irony, satire, sarcasm, ridicule. Their targets are pretense, pomposity, conformity, incompetence. And they'll tell you that their targets are everywhere and multiplying like Smurfs.

When I was a small boy, my father took me to the Stage Delicatessen in New York, having told me beforehand to keep my eyes open for "celebrities." By the time we were seated at a double table next to a tall, dour man, I had unsuccessfully scanned the place for Uncle Miltie or Captain Video or even Dagmar. Disappointed, I blurted out, "I don't see any *celebrities*!"

Our tablemate slowly looked up from his mushroom barley, and with his patented scowl, Fred Allen did a very, very slow burn in my direction. It was the dirtiest look I'd ever received, but I wasn't intimidated. Rather I felt that we had shared a joke, that I had been his straight man. He never let on, but I knew he was amused. My father introduced me to Mr. Fred Allen, and as he gently shook my hand without cracking a smile, I felt his unmistakable goodwill behind the curmudgeon's mask.

Curmudgeons are mockers and debunkers whose bitterness is a symptom rather than a disease. They can't compromise their standards and can't manage the suspension of disbelief necessary for feigned cheerfulness. Their awareness is a curse; they're constantly ticked off because they're constantly aware of so much to be ticked off about, and they wish things were better.

Perhaps curmudgeons have gotten a bad rap in the same way that the messenger is blamed for the message: They have the temerity to comment on the human condition without apology. They not only refuse to applaud mediocrity, they howl it down with morose glee. Their versions of the truth unsettle us, and we hold it against them, even though they soften it with humor.

H. L. Mencken was the quintessential curmudgeon, the one against whom all others must be measured. He wrote thirty books and countless essays, columns, and critical reviews. He was a lexicographer, reporter, and editor. He was the literary champion of Sherwood Anderson, Theodore Dreiser, Sinclair Lewis, and Eugene O'Neill.

He was the scourge of the middle class, which he called the "booboisie." In spite of his often condescending tone and lack of faith in his fellowman, he was a crusader against bigotry and injustice. He championed libertarianism and derided piety ("Puritanism is the haunting fear that someone, somewhere, may be happy"). He detested what he saw as the tyranny of the Fundamentalist Baptist Church of his day. If he were around today, he'd be all over Jerry Falwell.

The other great curmudgeons who have contributed to the general sanity of mankind— from Mark Twain and Ambrose Bierce to G. K. Chesterton and George Bernard Shaw, from Groucho Marx and W. C. Fields to John Simon and Paul Fussell— have all had the facility for recognizing and pointing out the absurdities of the human condition.

If there was a Golden Age of curmudgeonry, it was during the twenties and thirties at New York's Algonquin, an otherwise undistinguished hotel on West Forty-fourth Street. A dazzling array of wits and raconteurs gravitated to the table of Alexander Woollcott, the *New York Times* theater critic and book reviewer, and made it a bastion of urbanity and sparkling repartee. Edmund Wilson dubbed it an "all-star literary vaudeville." According to Groucho Marx, "The admission fee was a viper's tongue and a half-concealed stiletto. It was a sort of intellectual slaughterhouse." Clare Boothe Luce, no doubt because she was a frequent target of some of its members, was not amused: "You couldn't say 'Pass the salt' without somebody turning it into a pun or trying to top it."

The regulars among the artists, celebrities, and intellectuals who frequented the round table included Franklin P. Adams, Marc Connelly, George S. Kaufman, Harold Ross, Heywood Broun, Ring Lardner, Robert E. Sherwood, Robert Benchley, and Dorothy Parker. Other habitués included Oscar Levant, the Marx Brothers, Tallulah Bankhead, Herman Manckiewicz, Herbert Bayard Swope, Edna Ferber, Noel Coward, Charles MacArthur, and S. N. Behrman. As a result, the Algonquin Round Table is the single greatest source for the quotations and anecdotes in this book.

The pantheon of curmudgeonry is predominantly male, but a few women have earned the designation, most notably Dorothy Parker and Fran Lebowitz. Still, ninety percent are men, perhaps because until recently only men have had the opportunity for public spleen-venting.

The "featured" curmudgeons in these pages are not necessarily typical. Indeed, curmudgeons are fierce individualists by definition. Nevertheless, an examination of the lives of W. C. Fields, Karl Kraus, George S. Kaufman, Oscar Levant, Dorothy Parker, and Groucho Marx, reveals common threads. Many of them had unhappy childhoods and grew into neurotic, reclusive, self-centered adults. Many remained shy and insecure in spite of their celebrity. An inordinate number were prone to alcoholism, drug addiction, insomnia, hypochondria, mysogyny, even suicide.

The contemporary curmudgeons I interviewed displayed none of these tendencies. They're all intelligent, articulate, and personable. Many are happily married or mated; as far as I could tell, none hates women; and they all appeared healthy and sober when we met. They were unanimous in their reluctance to characterize themselves as curmudgeons without the proviso that anybody who *isn't* a curmudgeon nowadays simply is not paying attention. They were invariably forthright and responsive to my questions, both pertinent and impertinent. I'm grateful to all of them for their uncurmudgeonly cooperation.

You don't have to be a curmudgeon to make a curmudgeonly statement, so quotes from non- and quasi-curmudgeons are included herein—apparently even the terminally Pollyannish can have flashes of clarity. But the majority of the quotes in these pages are from the world-class curmudgeons listed on page 7.

I think I became a connoisseur of curmudgeons sometime in the early sixties, when I saw Oscar Levant in a series of television interviews with Jack Paar. Levant had been in and out of mental institutions ("I was once thrown out of a mental hospital for depressing the other patients"), was a mass of tics and twitches, and chain-smoked Newports (although his hands shook so badly, he needed help to light them). I was captivated by the twisted, toothless smile, the lucid mind within the degenerate body. (Paar: "What do you do for exercise?" Levant: "I stumble and then I fall into a coma.") Levant was at once pathetic and brilliant, witty and helpless, the essence of curmudgeonry in one enthralling package, a raw nerve of vulnerability eloquently lashing out at the sources of its torment.

By the early seventies I began to notice curmudgeonly tendencies in myself. I lost my tolerance for anything cute or trendy. I became increasingly out of step with everyone and everything around me. I developed a permanent sneer. I wrote fan letters to John Simon. I began to cultivate my surliness instead of trying to conceal it.

Eventually I gained the courage to come out of the closet, to go from an isolated, would-be iconoclast to an out-in-the-open curmudgeon. (Curmudgeons are like sumo wrestlers; it takes a long time and a lot of abuse to make one; curmudgeons are also like writers: you're a curmudgeon only when someone *else* says you're a curmudgeon.)

In short order I got an unlisted telephone number, enrolled in law school, divorced my wife, and managed to irreparably insult most of my friends and relatives. And I began collecting this material with the intention of someday compiling it in a book from which other closet curmudgeons might take solace. If it reaches just one other kindred soul and convinces him that there's no shame in chronic alienation, that curmudgeonry is a perfectly valid response to an increasingly exasperating world, it will have accomplished its goal.

J. W.
Pacific Palisades, California
March 1987

WORLD-CLASS CURMUDGEONS

GOODMAN ACE
FRED ALLEN
WOODY ALLEN
KINGSLEY AMIS
MATTHEW ARNOLD
TALLULAH BANKHEAD
JOHN BARRYMORE
LUCIUS BEEBE
MAX BEERBOHM
ROBERT BENCHLEY
AMBROSE BIERCE
ROY BLOUNT, JR.
JIMMY BRESLIN
HEYWOOD BROUN
WILLIAM F. BUCKLEY, JR.
TRUMAN CAPOTE
AL CAPP
G. K. CHESTERTON
QUENTIN CRISP
PETER DE VRIES
JULES FEIFFER
W. C. FIELDS
ANATOLE FRANCE
PAUL FUSSELL
ROBERT FROST
ALFRED HITCHCOCK
SAMUEL JOHNSON
BEN JONSON
GEORGE S. KAUFMAN
KARL KRAUS
STEPHEN LEACOCK
FRAN LEBOWITZ
OSCAR LEVANT

SAMUEL MARCHBANKS
GROUCHO MARX
H. L. MENCKEN
NANCY MITFORD
WILSON MIZNER
HENRY MORGAN
ROBERT MORLEY
VLADIMIR NABOKOV
GEORGE JEAN NATHAN
FRIEDRICH WILHELM
   NIETZSCHE
GEORGE ORWELL
DOROTHY PARKER
WESTBROOK PEGLER
S. J. PERELMAN
J. B. PRIESTLEY
ANDY ROONEY
MIKE ROYKO
MORT SAHL
GEORGE BERNARD SHAW
IAN SHOALES
JOHN SIMON
AUGUST STRINDBERG
CALVIN TRILLIN
MARK TWAIN
GORE VIDAL
VOLTAIRE
EVELYN WAUGH
OSCAR WILDE
BILLY WILDER
GEORGE F. WILL
EDMUND WILSON
ALEXANDER WOOLLCOTT

THE HEART
OF A CURMUDGEON

The believer is happy; the doubter is wise.
HUNGARIAN PROVERB

Men become civilized, not in proportion to their willingness to believe, but in proportion to their readiness to doubt. H. L. MENCKEN

To believe is very dull. To doubt is intensely engrossing. To be on the alert is to live, to be lulled into security is to die. OSCAR WILDE

Melancholy men, of all others, are the most witty.
ARISTOTLE

Real misanthropes are not found in solitude, but in the world; since it is experience of life, and not philosophy, which produces real hatred of mankind.
GIACOMO LEOPARDI

To knock a thing down, especially if it is cocked at an arrogant angle, is a deep delight of the blood.
GEORGE SANTAYANA

Every normal man must be tempted at times to
spit on his hands, hoist the black flag, and begin
slitting throats.   H. L. MENCKEN

Latent in every man is a venom of amazing bitterness, a black resentment; something that curses
and loathes life, a feeling of being trapped, of
having trusted and been fooled, of being the helpless prey of impotent rage, blind surrender, the
victim of a savage, ruthless power that gives and
takes away, enlists a man, drops him, promises
and betrays, and—crowning injury—inflicts on him
the humiliation of feeling sorry for himself.
                                    PAUL VALÉRY

There is no fate that cannot be surmounted by
scorn.   ALBERT CAMUS

Whoever is not a misanthrope at forty can never
have loved mankind.   NICOLAS CHAMFORT

A grouch escapes so many little annoyances that it
almost pays to be one.   KIN HUBBARD

A man gazing at the stars is proverbially at the
mercy of the puddles in the road.
                                ALEXANDER SMITH

QUOTES ON "A"

ABORTION

If men could get pregnant, abortion would be a
sacrament.   FLORYNCE KENNEDY

ABSTRACT ART

Abstract art: a product of the untalented sold by
the unprincipled to the utterly bewildered.

AL CAPP

ACQUAINTANCE

Acquaintance, *n.* A person whom we know well
enough to borrow from, but not well enough to
lend to.   AMBROSE BIERCE

ACTION

Action: the last resource of those who know not
how to dream.   OSCAR WILDE

If a thing is worth doing, it is worth doing badly.
G. K. CHESTERTON

ACTORS

I do not want actors and actresses to understand
my plays. That is not necessary. If they will only
pronounce the correct sounds I can guarantee the
results.   GEORGE BERNARD SHAW

Disney, of course, has the best casting. If he doesn't
like an actor, he just tears him up.
ALFRED HITCHCOCK

Some of the greatest love affairs I've known have involved one actor—unassisted. WILSON MIZNER

You can pick out actors by the glazed look that comes into their eyes when the conversation wanders away from themselves. MICHAEL WILDING

The scenery in the play was beautiful, but the actors got in front of it.
ALEXANDER WOOLLCOTT

The actor is not quite a human being—but then, who is? GEORGE SANDERS

Show me a great actor and I'll show you a lousy husband; show me a great actress, and you've seen the devil. W. C. FIELDS

An actor's success has the life expectancy of a small boy about to look into a gas tank with a lighted match. FRED ALLEN

Every actor has a natural animosity toward every other actor, present or absent, living or dead.
LOUISE BROOKS

Actors are crap. JOHN FORD

―――――――――― ADMIRATION ――――――――――

Admiration, *n*. Our polite recognition of another's resemblance to ourselves. AMBROSE BIERCE

―――――――――――― ADULT ――――――――――――

To be adult is to be alone. JEAN ROSTAND

Advertising may be described as the science of arresting human intelligence long enough to get money from it. STEPHEN LEACOCK

Advertising is 85 percent confusion and 15 percent commission. FRED ALLEN

Advertising is the rattling of a stick inside a swill bucket. GEORGE ORWELL

Advertising is a valuable economic factor because it is the cheapest way of selling goods, particularly if the goods are worthless. SINCLAIR LEWIS

Advertising is the modern substitute for argument; its function is to make the worse appear the better.
GEORGE SANTAYANA

Advertising is legalized lying. H. G. WELLS

————————————— ADVICE TO YOUNG WRITERS —————————————

Unless you think you can do better than Tolstoy, we don't need you. JAMES MICHENER

If a young writer can refrain from writing, he shouldn't hesitate to do so. ANDRÉ GIDE

————————————— AFFECTION —————————————

All my life, affection has been showered upon me, and every forward step I have made has been taken in spite of it. GEORGE BERNARD SHAW

Most affections are habits or duties we lack the courage to end. HENRI DE MONTHERLANT

The best years are the forties; after fifty a man begins to deteriorate, but in the forties he is at the maximum of his villainy.   H. L. MENCKEN

One of the delights known to age, and beyond the grasp of youth, is that of Not Going.

J. B. PRIESTLEY

_____ ALCOHOLIC _____

An alcoholic is someone you don't like who drinks as much as you do.   DYLAN THOMAS

_____ ALCOHOLISM _____

If the headache would only precede the intoxication, alcoholism would be a virtue.

SAMUEL BUTLER

_____ ALIMONY _____

Paying alimony is like feeding hay to a dead horse.

GROUCHO MARX

Judges, as a class, display, in the matter of arranging alimony, that reckless generosity which is found only in men who are giving away someone else's cash.   P. G. WODEHOUSE

Even hooligans marry, though they know that marriage is but for a little while. It is alimony that is forever.   QUENTIN CRISP

You never realize how short a month is until you pay alimony.   JOHN BARRYMORE

ALLIANCE

Alliance, *n*. In international politics, the union of two thieves who have their hands so deeply in each other's pocket that they cannot separately plunder a third. AMBROSE BIERCE

ALTRUISM

Every major horror of history was committed in the name of an altruistic motive. Has any act of selfishness ever equalled the carnage perpetrated by disciples of altruism? AYN RAND

Men are the only animals that devote themselves, day in and day out, to making one another unhappy. It is an art like any other. Its virtuosi are called altruists. H. L. MENCKEN

AMERICA

America is the only nation in history which miraculously has gone directly from barbarism to degeneration without the usual interval of civilization. GEORGES CLEMENCEAU

I have never been able to look upon America as young and vital, but rather as prematurely old, as a fruit which rotted before it had a chance to ripen. The word which gives the key to the national vice is waste. HENRY MILLER

In America, life is one long expectoration. OSCAR WILDE

An asylum for the sane would be empty in America.
GEORGE BERNARD SHAW

The civilization whose absence drove Henry James
to Europe.   GORE VIDAL

In our country we have those three unspeakably
precious things: freedom of speech, freedom of
conscience, and the prudence never to practice
either.   MARK TWAIN

In America sex is an obsession, in other parts of
the world it is a fact.   MARLENE DIETRICH

The only country in the world where failing to
promote yourself is regarded as being arrogant.
GARRY TRUDEAU

Every time Europe looks across the Atlantic to see
the American eagle, it observes only the rear end
of an ostrich.   AMBROSE BIERCE

The organization of American society is an inter-
locking system of semi-monopolies notoriously ve-
nal, an electorate notoriously unenlightened, misled
by a mass media notoriously phony.
PAUL GOODMAN

America . . . just a nation of two hundred million
used car salesmen with all the money we need to
buy guns and no qualms about killing anybody
else in the world who tries to make us uncomfortable.   HUNTER S. THOMPSON

America is the greatest of opportunities and the
worst of influences.   GEORGE SANTAYANA

In America, through pressure of conformity, there
is freedom of choice, but nothing to choose from.
                                        PETER USTINOV

> In America you can go on the air and kid the
> politicians, and the politicians can go on the air
> and kid the people.   GROUCHO MARX

The discovery of America was the occasion of the
greatest outburst of cruelty and reckless greed
known in history.   JOSEPH CONRAD

> America is still a government of the naive, by the
> naive, and for the naive. He who does not know
> this, nor relish it, has no inkling of the nature of
> this country.   CHRISTOPHER MORLEY

America is a mistake, a giant mistake!
                                        SIGMUND FREUD

_____ AMERICANS _____

> Americans are the only people in the world known
> to me whose status anxiety prompts them to ad-
> vertise their college and university affiliations in
> the rear window of their automobiles.
>   PAUL FUSSELL

When you consider how indifferent Americans are
to the quality and cooking of the food they put
into their insides, it cannot but strike you as pecu-
liar that they should take such pride in the mechanical appliances they use for its excretion.
                        W. SOMERSET MAUGHAM

Americans are like a rich father who wishes he knew how to give his son the hardships that made him rich.   ROBERT FROST

Americans can eat garbage, provided you sprinkle it liberally with ketchup, mustard, chili sauce, tabasco sauce, cayenne pepper, or any other condiment which destroys the original flavor of the dish.   HENRY MILLER

The genius of you Americans is that you never make clear-cut stupid moves, only complicated stupid moves which make us wonder at the possibility that there may be something to them which we are missing.   GAMAL ABDEL NASSER

The Americans are certainly great hero-worshipers, and always take their heroes from the criminal classes.   OSCAR WILDE

We don't know what we want, but we are ready to bite somebody to get it.   WILL ROGERS

I have defined the 100% American as 99% an idiot. And they just adore me.
                                    GEORGE BERNARD SHAW

Americans are broad-minded people. They'll accept the fact that a person can be an alcoholic, a dope fiend, a wife beater, and even a newspaperman, but if a man doesn't drive there's something wrong with him.   ART BUCHWALD

Americans are childish in many ways and about as subtle as a Wimpy burger; but in the long run it doesn't make any difference. They just turn on the power.   TOM WOLFE

──────────────── AMERICAN WAY ────────────────

The American way is to seduce a man by bribery and make a prostitute of him. Or else to ignore him, starve him into submission and make a hack out of him.   HENRY MILLER

──────────────── AMUSEMENT ────────────────

Amusement is the happiness of those who cannot think.   ALEXANDER POPE

──────────────── ANIMALS ────────────────

Animals have these advantages over man: they have no theologians to instruct them, their funerals cost them nothing, and no one starts lawsuits over their wills.   VOLTAIRE

──────────────── APPLAUSE ────────────────

This strange beating together of hands has no meaning. To me it is very disturbing. We try to make sounds like music, and then in between comes this strange sound.   LEOPOLD STOKOWSKI

──────────────── AQUARIUM ────────────────

There is something about a home aquarium which sets my teeth on edge the moment I see it. Why anyone would want to live with a small container

of stagnant water populated by a half-dead guppy
is beyond me.   S. J. PERELMAN

ARCHBISHOP

Archbishop: a Christian ecclesiastic of a rank superior to that attained by Christ.   H. L. MENCKEN

ART

Without art, the crudeness of reality would make
the world unbearable.   GEORGE BERNARD SHAW

If more than ten percent of the population likes a
painting it should be burned, for it must be bad.
GEORGE BERNARD SHAW

ATTLEE, CLEMENT

He is a sheep in sheep's clothing.
WINSTON CHURCHILL

Mr. Attlee is a very modest man. But then he has
much to be modest about.
WINSTON CHURCHILL

AUTOBIOGRAPHY

Autobiography is an unrivalled vehicle for telling
the truth about other people.   PHILIP GUEDALLA

AWARDS

Awards are merely the badges of mediocrity.
CHARLES IVES

Nothing would disgust me more, morally, than receiving an Oscar. LUIS BUÑUEL

This medal [the National Book Award], together with my American Express Card, will identify me worldwide—except at Bloomingdale's.
S. J. PERELMAN

It [the Legion of Honor] is taken rather seriously by those who have received it.
ALFRED HITCHCOCK

Awards are like hemorrhoids; in the end, every asshole gets one. FREDERIC RAPHAEL

H. L. MENCKEN

Stirring Up the Animals

HENRY LOUIS MENCKEN was born in Baltimore on September 12, 1880, the eldest of four children of a middle-class German-American family. He had a happy, secure, normal childhood: He described himself as "a larva of the comfortable and complacent bourgeoisie" and wrote that "we were encapsulated in affection and kept fat, saucy and contented."

His father owned and managed a cigar factory and imbued his son with a belief in the efficacy of independent action and thought, and instilled in him a love of reading. There was a modest library in the Mencken home, and the young Harry, as he was called, obtained a reader's card at Baltimore's Pratt Library at the age of nine. It was there that he discovered *Huckleberry Finn,* an event he would later characterize as 'the most stupendous of my whole life."

He attended the Baltimore Polytechnic and went into the family business upon graduation but soon grew dissatisfied with his job and wanted to quit to become a newspaperman. When his father died in 1899, his uncle assumed control of the factory and Mencken was free to pursue a career in journalism. He immediately obtained a series of trial reporting assignments from the Baltimore *Morning Herald,* and within a few months, at the age of eighteen, he became the youngest reporter on the staff. By 1903 he had become city editor, and in 1905 he became the editor of the *Evening Herald.* He moved to the famous Baltimore *Sun* papers in 1906, first as a member of the staff of the *Morning Sun* and then of the *Evening Sun.*

He became literary critic of *The Smart Set* in 1908. His "Free Lance" column in the Baltimore *Evening Sun,* which first appeared in 1910, influenced journalists all over the country with its vibrant, iconoclastic approach to the issues of the time.

In 1914, he became coeditor of *The Smart Set* with George Jean Nathan. In their first issue they published the following credo: "Our policy is to be lively without being nasty. On the one hand, no smut, and on the other, nothing uplifting. A magazine for civilized adults in their lighter moods." In 1924, Mencken became the editor of *The American Mercury* where he published and supported such young American writers as Sinclair Lewis, James Branch Cabell, and Theodore Dreiser.

H. L. Mencken became one of the most influential and prolific American social critics of the first half of the twentieth century, reaching the peak of his influence and popularity in the twenties. His perennial target was American society, with which he maintained a love-hate relationship all his life. In "Catechism," he anticipated the inevitable question: "Q: If you find so much that is unworthy of reverence in the United States, then why do you live here? A: Why do men go to zoos?"

He considered emotion the enemy of intelligence and tried to hold it at bay whenever possible, a conviction that formed one of the underpinnings of his individualistic, aristocratic worldview. He held pomposity, incompetence, and pedantry in utter contempt. He believed, above all else, in the freedom to speak one's mind about anything at any time.

Mencken abominated Baptists and Methodists and delighted in skewering them in print, a practice that earned him the sobriquet "The Anti-Christ of Baltimore." But he wasn't anti-Christ, just anti-Christian, though he would have applauded the implementation of the teachings of Christ by Christians. He detested radio and television, abhorred liberals and the "Tory plutocracy," the rabble and the "uplifters" alike. He considered himself a spokesman for the "civilized minority" and attacked anything he deemed inimical to the freedom of the artist. He once described his function as "stirring up the animals."

Mencken had an abiding contempt for economists and economics. When he learned that President Franklin Delano Roosevelt (whom he called "Roosevelt Minor") had devalued the dollar, Mencken erupted in print, calling the measure downright robbery. He even briefly considered bringing legal action against the government. No sooner had he calmed down than the Supreme Court "packing" controversy exploded, sealing his opinion of "Roosevelt Minor" forever and marking the beginning of the decline in Mencken's influence. When Hitler came to power in Germany, Mencken didn't take him seriously and failed to attack him vigorously enough for many of his readers, who denounced Mencken as a Nazi and an anti-Semite.

He was one of our most distinguished and prolific men of letters. Walter Lippmann called him "the most powerful personal influence on this whole generation of educated people." His literary output consisted of thirty books, countless essays and reviews, and voluminous correspondence. It has been estimated that he wrote five thousand words a day for forty years. He was a prodigious reader and probably had one of the largest vocabularies of any American writer. He coined many neologisms, most notably *Bible Belt, booboisie, smuthound,* and *Boobus americanus.*

The American Language, his monumental study of American English, was first published in 1919 and went through several editions and supplements. It demonstrated conclusively for the first time that American English was a separate entity from its British progenitor. His critical essays were collected in the six-volume *Prejudices,* and his autobiographical essays were collected in *Happy Days, Newspaper Days,* and *Heathen Days.*

He led a cheerful, active, gregarious private life. He enjoyed hearty food, good pilsner, and the company of women. Contrary to his oft-expressed sentiments on marriage (i.e., "If I ever marry, it will be on a sudden impulse—as a man shoots himself"), in 1930, he surprised his friends and readers by marrying a beautiful Goucher College instructor named Sara Powell Haardt. Though her health was poor from the outset, they lived happily together for five years until her death from tuberculosis in 1935. He mourned her loss deeply, yet was able to say to a friend, "When I married Sara the doctors said she would not live more than three years. Actually she lived five, so I had two more years of happiness than I had any right to expect."

Henry Louis Mencken died on January 29, 1956, eight years after a massive stroke had rendered him virtually aphasic. That he was deprived of his ability to read and write was a grotesque irony that wasn't lost on Mencken himself: shortly before Mencken's death, a visitor mentioned the name of a mutual acquaintance who had died in 1948. Mencken thought for a moment and finally said, "Ah, yes, he died the same year I did."

MENCKEN'S AMERICA

The United States, to my eye, is incomparably the greatest show on earth . . . we have clowns among us who are as far above the clowns of any other great state as Jack Dempsey is above the paralytic— and not a few dozen or score of them, but whole droves and herds.

Nowhere in the world is superiority more easily attained, or more eagerly admitted. The chief business of the nation, as a nation, is the setting up of heroes, mainly bogus.

The American people, taking one with another, constitute the most timorous, sniveling, poltroonish, ignominious mob of serfs and goose-steppers ever gathered under one flag in Christendom since the end of the Middle Ages.

There's no underestimating the intelligence of the American public.

The typical American of today has lost all the love of liberty that his forefathers had, and all their disgust of emotion, and pride in self-reliance. He is led no longer by Davy Crocketts; he is led by cheer leaders, press agents, word-mongers, uplifters.

Perhaps the most revolting character that the United States ever produced was the Christian business man.

———

I simply can't imagine competence as anything save admirable, for it is very rare in this world, and especially in this great Republic, and those who have it in some measure, in any art or craft from adultery to zoology, are the only human beings I can think of who will be worth the oil it will take to fry them in Hell.

———

The only way to success in American public life lies in flattering and kowtowing to the mob.

———

Congress consists of one-third, more or less, scoundrels; two-thirds, more or less, idiots; and three-thirds, more or less, poltroons.

———

Democracy is the art of running the circus from the monkey cage.

———

This place [Hollywood] is the true and original arse-hole of creation. The movie dogs, compared with the rest of the population, actually seem like an ancient Italian noblesse.

Democracy is the theory that the common people know what they want, and deserve to get it good and hard.

———————

Democracy is grounded upon so childish a complex of fallacies that they must be protected by a rigid system of taboos, else even halfwits would argue it to pieces. Its first concern must thus be to penalize the free play of ideas.

———————

In this world of sin and sorrow there is always something to be thankful for; as for me, I rejoice that I am not a Republican.

———————

The California climate makes the sick well and the well sick, the old young and the young old.

———————

In Southern California the vegetables have no flavor and the flowers have no smell.

———————

Los Angeles seems an inconceivably shoddy place . . . a pasture foreordained for the cow-town evangelism of a former sideshow wriggler.

———————

[Los Angeles:] Nineteen suburbs in search of a metropolis.

Maine is as dead, intellectually, as Abyssinia. Nothing is ever heard from it.

The New England shopkeepers and theologians never really developed a civilization; all they ever developed was a government. They were, at their best, tawdry and tacky fellows, oafish in manner and devoid of imagination.

New York: A third-rate Babylon.

The trouble with New York is that it has no nationality at all. It is simply a sort of free port—a place where the raw materials of civilization are received, sorted out, and sent further on.

For all its size and all its wealth and all the "progress" it babbles of, it [the South] is almost as sterile, artistically, intellectually, culturally, as the Sahara Desert.

[Texas is] the place where there are the most cows and the least milk and the most rivers and the least water in them, and where you can look the farthest and see the least.

QUOTES ON "B"

BABY

A soiled baby, with a neglected nose, cannot be conscientiously regarded as a thing of beauty.

MARK TWAIN

I find that the most successful approach to the subject of babies is to discuss them as though they were hams; the firmness of the flesh, the pinkness of the flesh, the even distribution of fat, the sweetness and tenderness of the whole, and the placing of bone are the things to praise.

SAMUEL MARCHBANKS

BACHELORS

Rich bachelors should be heavily taxed. It is not fair that some men should be happier than others.

OSCAR WILDE

BALLET

Ballet is the fairies' baseball.   OSCAR LEVANT

BANK

A bank is a place where they lend you an umbrella in fair weather and ask for it back when it begins to rain.   ROBERT FROST

BANKHEAD, TALLULAH

A day away from Tallulah is like a month in the country.   HOWARD DIETZ

_____

_____ BARRETT, RONA _____

She doesn't need a steak knife. Rona cuts her food
with her tongue.   JOHNNY CARSON

_____ BASEBALL _____

Baseball has the great advantage over cricket of
being sooner ended.   GEORGE BERNARD SHAW

_____ BEAUTY _____

I'm tired of all this nonsense about beauty being
only skin-deep. That's deep enough. What do you
want, an adorable pancreas?   JEAN KERR

_____ BEGGARS _____

Beggars should be abolished. It annoys one to
give to them, and it annoys one not to give to
them.   FRIEDRICH WILHELM NIETZSCHE

_____ BELIEF _____

The most costly of all follies is to believe passion-
ately in the palpably not true. It is the chief occupation of mankind.   H. L. MENCKEN

If there were a verb meaning "to believe falsely," it
would not have any significant first person, present indicative.   LUDWIG WITTGENSTEIN

_____ BEST-SELLER _____

A best-seller is the gilded tomb of a mediocre
talent.   LOGAN PEARSALL SMITH

_____

—————————————————— BET ——————————————————

It may be that the race is not always to the swift,
nor the battle to the strong—but that is the way
to bet.   DAMON RUNYON

—————————————— BEVERLY HILLS ——————————————

If you stay in Beverly Hills too long you become a
Mercedes.   ROBERT REDFORD

—————————————————— BIBLE ——————————————————

"The Good Book"—one of the most remarkable
euphemisms ever coined.   ASHLEY MONTAGU

It ain't those parts of the Bible that I can't understand that bother me, it's the parts that I do
understand.   MARK TWAIN

The Bible tells us to love our neighbors, and also
to love our enemies; probably because they are
generally the same people.   G. K. CHESTERTON

So far as I can remember, there is not one word
in the Gospels in praise of intelligence.
                                        BERTRAND RUSSELL

Scriptures, n. The sacred books of our holy religion, as distinguished from the false and profane
writings on which all other faiths are based.
                                          AMBROSE BIERCE

The inspiration of the Bible depends on the ignorance of the gentleman who reads it.
                                        ROBERT G. INGERSOLL

BIGAMY

Bigamy is having one wife too many. Monogamy is the same.   OSCAR WILDE

BIRD-WATCHING

I am the kind of man who would never notice an oriole building a nest unless it came and built it in my hat in the hat room of the club.

STEPHEN LEACOCK

BIRTH

No one recovers from the disease of being born, a deadly wound if there ever was one.

E. M. CIORAN

BLOODSHED

I must apologize for the lack of bloodshed in tonight's program. We shall try to do better next time.   ALFRED HITCHCOCK

BOOKS

Books are fatal: they are the curse of the human race. Nine-tenths of existing books are nonsense, and the clever books are the refutation of that nonsense. The greatest misfortune that ever befell man was the invention of printing.

BENJAMIN DISRAELI

Books for general reading always smell badly. The odor of common people hangs about them.

FRIEDRICH WILHELM NIETZSCHE

The multitude of books is making us ignorant.
VOLTAIRE

I have given up reading books; I find it takes my
mind off myself.　　　OSCAR LEVANT

―――――――――――――― BORE ――――――――――――――

Bore, *n*. A person who talks when you wish him
to listen.　　　AMBROSE BIERCE

Bore: a man who is never unintentionally rude.
OSCAR WILDE

He is not only dull himself, he is the cause of
dullness in others.　　　SAMUEL JOHNSON

Bores bore each other too, but it never seems to
teach them anything.　　　DON MARQUIS

We often forgive those who bore us, but we cannot forgive those whom we bore.
FRANÇOIS DE LA ROCHEFOUCAULD

A bore is a fellow talking who can change the
subject back to his topic of conversation faster
than you can change it back to yours.
LAURENCE J. PETER

―――――――――― BORN-AGAIN CHRISTIANS ――――――――――

The trouble with born-again Christians is that they
are an even bigger pain the second time around.
HERB CAEN

He's a born-again Christian. The trouble is, he suffered brain damage during rebirth.

ANONYMOUS

BOSTON

I have just returned from Boston. It is the only thing to do if you find yourself up there.

FRED ALLEN

BOURGEOIS

To have a horror of the bourgeois is bourgeois.

JULES RENARD

BOY

The fact that boys are allowed to exist at all is evidence of a remarkable Christian forebearance among men.

AMBROSE BIERCE

Boys are capital fellows in their own way, among their mates; but they are unwholesome companions for grown people.

CHARLES LAMB

BREAKFAST

Only dull people are brilliant at breakfast.

OSCAR WILDE

My wife and I tried two or three times in the last forty years to have breakfast together, but it was so disagreeable we had to stop.

WINSTON CHURCHILL

_____

_____ **BREVITY** _____

Brevity is the soul of lingerie. DOROTHY PARKER

_____ **BRIDE** _____

Brides aren't happy—they are just triumphant.
JOHN BARRYMORE

Hollywood brides keep the bouquets and throw
away the grooms. GROUCHO MARX

Bride, *n*. A woman with a fine prospect of happiness behind her. AMBROSE BIERCE

_____ **BROADWAY** _____

What a glorious garden of wonders the lights of
Broadway would be to anyone lucky enough to be
unable to read. G. K. CHESTERTON

_____ **BROTHERHOOD** _____

The brotherhood of man is not a mere poet's
dream: it is a most depressing and humiliating
reality. OSCAR WILDE

It's silly to go on pretending that under the skin
we are all brothers. The truth is more likely that
under the skin we are all cannibals, assassins, trai-
tors, liars, hypocrites, poltroons. HENRY MILLER

_____ **BUREAUCRACY** _____

Bureaucracy is a giant mechanism operated by
pygmies. HONORÉ DE BALZAC

_____

The Vicar of Vitriol Loves Animals

JOHN SIMON is one of America's foremost critics of the arts. He is the drama critic for *New York* magazine, the film critic for the *National Review,* and the author of ten books of criticism. He has written extensively on the uses and abuses of the English language, most conspicuously in the best-selling *Paradigms Lost.*

He was born in Subotica, Yugoslavia, in 1925. He emigrated to the United States in 1941 and served with the U.S. Army Air

Corps during World War II. He was a Fulbright fellow at the University of Paris in 1949 and received a Ph.D. from Harvard in 1959. He taught at MIT and Bard College before joining the *Hudson Review* as its drama critic in 1960. He's been the drama and cultural critic for *The New Leader,* drama critic for *Commonweal,* and drama and language critic for *Esquire.*

JW: *When you walked in, you complained about not receiving any hate mail. Do you really like it?*

JS: So much mail that one gets tends to be silly, so one would rather be attacked in it than praised. Which is not to say that it isn't pleasurable to receive a well-written, well-thought-out letter that praises one. But when you get a totally illiterate letter, it might as well be a hate letter so you can at least get a laugh out of it.

JW: *Do you consider yourself a curmudgeon?*

JS: No, only because it's a funny word. Nobody even knows exactly where it comes from. If you check into its etymology, it may come from an old Scottish word which means something like murmur, or mumble, or grumble. There's a popular etymology which says it comes from *coeur mechant,* but there's no scientific basis for that. Anyway, it's not a word that I would apply to myself because why should I laugh at myself? Let others say it if they wish. If you said *misanthrope,* I would say—well, yes—but then look at humanity. And what other word might you use? If you were to say *elitist,* it might be accurate, because in this society to be an elitist is almost automatically to be a curmudgeon.

JW: *A cynic?*
JS: Well, again, a cynic is more like a curmudgeon or a misanthrope—not something that one instinctually is, not something that one wants to be, but something that circumstances force one into. I would distinguish between people who are by *temperament* that way and people who have been soured into becoming that way, though the end result may be similar.
JW: *Where do you place yourself in those terms?*
JS: I did not have curmudgeonliness thrust upon me, but if I have it, it evolved gradually as a response to having to see so many bad plays and movies and review so many bad books. It's not something that I profess with pride or joy, it's just an attitude that becomes less and less resistible under the circumstances.

In my case it is almost always said that I'm a curmudgeon because of my reviews, and to me that is particularly nonsensical because criticism is not meant to be the Red Cross or the Salvation Army. To me it is proof of the uncultivatedness of this society that it boggles at severe criticism.

The trouble is, the society is geared to blandness. Blandness is a curse, as I see it. It's shapeless, it's savorless, it's mindless, it's gutless.
JW: *I'd like to run down a list of subjects, things that have bothered curmudgeons. Children, for example.*
JS: Babies on airplanes that howl all through the flight I certainly do *not* approve of. There should be special baby compartments. I think they should put the cigarette smokers and babies together and see who drives the other crazy quicker.

JW: *Do you have anything against hunting?*

JS: I don't like it. I love animals. I suppose you can't outlaw it, and I suppose there are certain species that need decimation now and again, but when some very beautiful creatures are killed for their fur or their plumage, or just for the alleged glory of it, I think it's disgusting.

JW: *How do you react to religious fundamentalists?*

JS: They're good people to debate on television or radio but that's the only use I have for them. As for born-again Christians, it seems to me that on the whole, one birth per person is enough, and for some even that may be too much.

JW: *You've written extensively on the state of the language. I even remember seeing you debate a woman about it on television . . .*

JS: Geneva Smitherman, or "Smitherperson" as I like to call her. Her stock has not only fallen, it has disappeared. That was about ten years ago.

JW: *Has the language deteriorated since then?*

JS: You don't have to wait ten years—ten seconds is enough. Every day in the *Times,* which is supposed to be our best newspaper, you find more errors, and *grosser* errors, and that's a telling index to what's going on everywhere. The talk I hear among civilized people, which used to be fairly grammatical until about twelve or fifteen years ago, has now gone completely to pot.

JW: *Do you think there's any relationship between this trend and what George Orwell warned about in "Politics and the English Language" or what Karl Kraus railed against: a conspiracy of journalism, govern-*

ment, and industry to erode our linguistic sensibilities in order to control us?

JS (*laughs*): I must say that the things Karl Kraus was railing against were much better than the things being held up as examples of good usage today. But yes, I imagine, *grosso modo,* that these are all parts of the same ongoing process of deterioration. The worst part of it is that there are all these pseudophilosophical and political justifications for the deterioration. Now if terrible grammar is used, it's justified by liberal or leftist politics: it's everybody's political right to speak as abominably as he or she wishes. There's an organized pull towards undermining the language whether it's by feminists, homosexuals, or some ethnic minority whose attempts to undermine English are considered their God-given or state-given right. I'm not for conformity for its own sake, I'm for using language imaginatively, but imaginatively does not mean incorrectly. In fact, it's very easy to be imaginative if you are incorrect: If you tie your necktie around your knee instead of around your neck, you are imaginative, but you are imaginative in an imbecile way.

It's true anywhere: A director like Peter Sellars takes a play and makes hash out of it. If people are supposed to walk somewhere because it's part of the play, he puts them in a helicopter; if someone is supposed to lie down in a bed, he has him float off in some kind of contraption just to be different. That is not imaginativeness, that is junk.

JW: *Is that how we arrive at "dinner theater"?*

JS: Dinner theater is reducing art to a commodity in the worst way. It's by definition junk. You won't see *Macbeth* at a dinner theater. Dinner theater is anti-culture. Start people on the idea that theater is something you can *eat at,* and next thing you're at a play and someone is shaking the ice in a cup of Coca Cola all through the performance and you can't hear. Who wants to be surrounded by food containers in a theater?

JW: *People seem to be talking more in the theater.*

JS: Yes, and it's generally ascribed to the influence of television. You watch it in your living room where you throw beer cans around and make funny remarks and go to the toilet and flush it noisily while the show is on. God knows television has something bad to do with almost everything, so why not that? But I think it's worse than that; I think it's a falling off in manners. Manners are one of the truly lost causes.

JW: *What's the cause of this deterioration of manners?*

JS: Bad manners are socially inevitable because as the lower orders become more affluent, which God knows no one begrudges them, they come into situations in which they don't know how to behave. Nothing in their training has prepared them for it.

JW: *Is it a case of diminishing attention spans?*

JS: Yes, yes. More and more ways are being devised to make concentration a thing of the past. Concentration becomes more and more like an appendix or a tail, useless organs we lost long ago.

The way painters paint today, you don't have to know anything about painting. Once you admit Jackson Pollock to the ranks of great painters, anybody can paint; once junk can be sculpture, anybody can be a sculptor. The difficulty is being taken out of everything and as a result the riffraff takes over.

JW: *Would "performance art" be an extreme example of this?*

JS: Performance art is nonsense. It's something that anybody without any training, any culture, or any genius can do. If it's bizarre enough, it works. If it's bizarre, it's art. We're back to the necktie around the knee.

JW: *What about punk rock?*

JS: It's disgusting, it's revolting, it's sheer aggressive sickness, but I don't waste my time fulminating against it because what's the use? What bothers me more than punk rock is supposedly "intellectual rock." When people start telling me that Talking Heads is something very special or when some reputable critic tells me that Dylan is a great poet, that's when my dander is up, because I think it's all junk.

JW: *How have you adjusted to your own visibility, your own celebrity? Do you enjoy being recognized?*

JS: I'm often recognized but not by the right people. An ex-girlfriend of mine said, "Have you noticed that the people who come up to you in public places and gush about your work are almost always creeps?"

JW: *Does Christmas annoy you?*

JS: Yes, Christmas is a problem. If it were confined to just a few days, okay, but Christmas keeps moving sinisterly forward, or backward, depending from which angle you're looking at it, so that when they start in July with Christmas shopping, or Christmas planning, or Christmas this and that, it's nauseating.

JW: *The family has been a perennial target for curmudgeons.*

JS: Yes, one ought to be able to choose those that one is close to. If I like you, I want you as my friend; if I don't like you, I don't want you as my friend—it's that simple. In a family, of course, you don't have that choice, and yet you're forced into closeness with people. It's a curse. If you have an enormous nose, I suppose you can have an operation to make it smaller, but you can't operate away an undesirable family member.

JW: *You've talked a lot about your dislike of smoking.*

JS: Smoking I find a disgusting habit. If it were just deleterious for the people who do it, I'd say fine, let them kill themselves, but unfortunately it bothers me and affects my health. And it produces a disgusting smell and creates dirt and burns holes in things, good things; it starts fires in hotels. I find it an absolutely beastly habit.

JW: *Are you encouraged by the trend toward banning smoking in public places?*

JS: Smoking should be forbidden in all public places, and people should be allowed to say, "I'm giving a small dinner party but I am allergic to smoke, so if you can't live without smoking, don't come."

JW: *Do you attend many literary parties?*

JS: The problem is, we don't have enough literature to justify all the parties given in its name. Anyway, I don't get invited to many, which may or may not have something to do with my curmudgeonliness. But that's fine because I prefer non-literary parties as long as they're not illiterate.

JW: *Do you really hate actors?*

JS: There are good actors and bad actors, and needless to say, I prefer the good ones, but socially speaking, with the exception of a few Europeans and a very few Americans, actors are basically an uncultured, uncivilized, pretentious lot.

JW: *Does that include Ronald Reagan?*

JS: Well, you could say that his acting wasn't very serious and that he could just as easily have become a sports announcer; he was not an actor in the sense that Marlon Brando is an actor (or *was* an actor). Still, acting is not a profession from which I would want my governments to originate.

JW: *How do you feel about Teddy Kennedy?*

JS: I don't like people who use up good-looking young women in such a way that they end up at the bottom of rivers or lakes. Nor do I particularly care for people who cheat on their exams at Harvard. Nor do I particularly like obesity, and he's gotten very obese. Other than that, I have no special feeling about him one way or the other.

JW: *You don't have to be a curmudgeon to dislike lawyers. What's your opinion of them?*

JS: There's nothing implicit in being a lawyer that means you have to be boring or repulsive or brash. Certainly, when a man like Alan Dershowitz comes along, it makes you want to go out and stone a few lawyers, preferably *him,* but there aren't that many Dershowitzes, thank God. I've known some perfectly nice lawyers and some not-so-nice ones. *Women* lawyers are a separate problem. There's something about the law that makes women unfeminine, and despite what the feminists and homosexuals say, a woman should be feminine and a man should be masculine.

JW: *Do you agree with feminists that pornography exploits women?*

JS: Pornography serves a perfectly legitimate use: It's trashily enjoyable, essentially harmless, and a safety valve. Of course, there's good pornography and bad pornography—but to go out and militate against it in some passionate, fanatical way I find misguided. It's a legitimate outlet for otherwise frustrated sexuality, and if somebody reads a pornographic magazine or novel or sees a pornographic movie, I don't see any harm in it, generally speaking. Whereas I do see harm in all these self-righteous people crusading for this worthy cause because it supposedly exploits women: They end up being censors. If they're so concerned about it, women should write bigger and better pornography of their own and start exploiting men. Of course, it's another thing when it involves or reaches children; I'm not in favor of exposing any unformed mind to it. And I personally wish, even where consenting adults are involved, that it would not involve bloodletting.

Pornography, like anything else, may occasionally have harmful effects. Occasionally a sexual crime may have some connection with pornography, but for all attempts to do so, this has never been conclusively demonstrated. Anything can be harmful if it falls into the wrong hands. A baseball bat is not in itself a bad thing, but it can be used as a weapon in the commission of a crime. Are we then to ban baseball? I think not.

PARAMOURS LOST: JOHN SIMON ON ASSORTED ACTRESSES

LINDA BLAIR, not a very talented or prepossessing youngster then, is even less interesting now, though considerably more bovine; I doubt whether a post-pubertal acting style can be made out of mere chubbiness.

DYAN CANNON, as Julie [in *Such Good Friends*], exudes a stupidity that strikes me uncomfortably as the actress's own contribution to the part; her one true talent is for bitchiness, a rather lowly gift.

DORIS DAY: The only ... talent Miss Day possesses is that of being absolutely sanitary: her personality untouched by human emotions, her brow unclouded by human thought, her form unsmudged by the slightest evidence of femininity.

SANDY DENNIS: Pauline Kael has aptly observed that Miss Dennis "has made an acting style out of postnasal drip." It should be added that she balanced her postnasal condition with something like prefrontal lobotomy, so that when she is not a walking catarrh she is a blithering imbecile.

SHELLY DUVALL is the worst and homeliest thing to hit the movies since Liza Minnelli.

JUDY GARLAND: Her figure resembles the giant economy-size tube of toothpaste in girls' bathrooms: squeezed intemperately at all points, it acquires a shape that defies definition by the most resourceful solid geometrician.

KATHARINE HEPBURN: When you think of the great Marguerite Moreno, who created the role [of Aurelia in *The Madwoman of Chaillot*], and then look at this performance, exact replicas of which have already earned Miss Hepburn two ill-deserved Oscars, you may wish to forsake the auditorium for the vomitorium.

CAROL KANE: You have to have a stomach for ugliness to endure Carol Kane—to say nothing of the zombielike expressions she mistakes for acting.

ANGELA LANSBURY: God only knows where the notion that Miss Lansbury has class originated; perhaps her vestigial lower-middle-class English accent passes for that in our informed show-biz circles. She is, in fact, common; and her mugging, rattling-off or steam-rollering across her lines, and camping around merely make her into that most degraded thing an *outré* actress can decline into: a fag hag.

DIANE KEATON . . . is yet another of those non-actresses this country produces in such abundance—women who trade on the raw materials of their neuroses, which has nothing to do with acting.

Her work, if that is the word for it, always consists chiefly of a dithering, blithering, neurotic coming apart at the seams—an acting style that is really a nervous breakdown in slow-motion.

ALI MACGRAW: Miss MacGraw cannot act at all. At the screening [of *The Getaway*] I attended, people were laughing out loud at her delivery of lines—rather like a grade-school pupil asking to be excused to go to the bathroom.

MELINA MERCOURI: As for Miss Mercouri, her blackly mascaraed eye-sockets gape like twin craters, unfortunately extinct.

LIZA MINNELLI: That turnipy nose overhanging a forward-gaping mouth and hastily retreating chin, that bulbous cranium with eyes as big (and as inexpressive) as saucers; those are the appurtenances of a clown—a funny clown, not even a sad one . . . Miss Minnelli has only two things going for her: a father and a mother who got there in the first place, and tasteless reviewers and audiences who keep her there.

CHARLOTTE RAMPLING [is] a poor actress who mistakes creepiness for sensuality.

DIANA RIGG is built like a brick mausoleum with insufficient flying buttresses.

CYBILL SHEPHERD: If it weren't for an asinine superciliousness radiating from her, Miss Shepherd would actually be pitiable, rather like a kid from an orphanage trying to play Noel Coward. In fact, she comes across like one of those inanimate objects, say, a cupboard or a grandfather clock, which is made in certain humorous shorts to act, through trick photography, like people.

BARBRA STREISAND: Miss Streisand looks like a cross between an aardvark and an albino rat surmounted by a platinum-coated horse bun. Though she has good eyes and a nice complexion, the rest of her is a veritable anthology of disaster areas. Her speaking voice seems to have graduated from the Brooklyn Conservatory of Yentaism, and her acting consists entirely of fishily thrusting out her lips, sounding like a cabbie bellyaching at breakneck speed, and throwing her weight around.

ELIZABETH TAYLOR: Miss Taylor . . . has grown so ample that it has become necessary to dress her almost exclusively in a variety of ambulatory tents. On the few occasions when she does reveal her bosom (or part thereof) [in *The Sandpiper*], one breast (or part thereof) proves sufficient to traverse an entire wide-screen frame—diagonally.

BRENDA VACCARO: With the exception of Sandy Dennis, there is no more irritatingly unfeminine actress around these days than Miss Vaccaro, a cube-shaped creature who comes across as a dikey Kewpie doll.

THE CRITICAL CURMUDGEON

With the single exception of Homer, there is no eminent writer, not even Sir Walter Scott, whom I can despise so entirely as I despise Shakespeare, when I measure my mind against his.

GEORGE BERNARD SHAW

Now we sit through Shakespeare in order to recognize the quotations.

OSCAR WILDE

Hamlet is a coarse and barbarous play . . . One might think the work is a product of a drunken savage's imagination.

VOLTAIRE

Hamlet has been played by 5,000 actors—no wonder he is crazy.

H. L. MENCKEN

Are the commentators on *Hamlet* really mad, or only pretending to be?

OSCAR WILDE

He had one of the more wicked minds ever going.

TRUMAN CAPOTE on Mark Twain

Mr. Henry James writes fiction as if it were a painful duty.

OSCAR WILDE

One must have a heart of stone to read the death
of Little Nell by Dickens without laughing.

OSCAR WILDE

He festooned the dung heap on which he had
placed himself with sonnets as people grow hon-
eysuckle around outdoor privies.

QUENTIN CRISP on Oscar Wilde

You have to be over thirty to enjoy Proust.

GORE VIDAL

He became mellow before he became ripe.

ALEXANDER WOOLLCOTT on Christopher Morley

Bernard Shaw has no enemies but is intensely
disliked by his friends.   OSCAR WILDE

It is his life work to announce the obvious in
terms of the scandalous.

H. L. MENCKEN on George Bernard Shaw

Mr. Shaw is (I suspect) the only man on earth
who has never written any poetry.

G. K. CHESTERTON

He writes his plays for the ages—the ages between five and twelve.
GEORGE JEAN NATHAN on George Bernard Shaw

His style has the desperate jauntiness of an orchestra fiddling away for dear life on a sinking ship.
EDMUND WILSON on Evelyn Waugh

If it must be Thomas, let it be Mann, and if it must be Wolfe let it be Nero, but never let it be Thomas Wolfe.
PETER DE VRIES

Odets, where is thy sting?   GEORGE S. KAUFMAN

He is a bad novelist and a fool. The combination usually makes for great popularity in the U.S.
GORE VIDAL on Alexander Solzhenitsyn

Capote should be heard, not read.   GORE VIDAL

Truman Capote has made lying an art. A *minor* art.
GORE VIDAL

That's not writing, that's typing.
                    TRUMAN CAPOTE on Jack Kerouac

He's a second-rate Stephen Birmingham. And Stephen Birmingham is third-rate.
                    TRUMAN CAPOTE on Louis Auchincloss

The House Beautiful is the play lousy.
                    DOROTHY PARKER

Perfectly Scandalous was one of those plays in which all of the actors unfortunately enunciated very clearly.
                    ROBERT BENCHLEY

Number Seven opened last night. It was misnamed by five.
                    ALEXANDER WOOLLCOTT

There's less here than meets the eye.
                    TALLULAH BANKHEAD on a Maeterlinck play

Ouch!   WOLCOTT GIBBS reviewing *Wham!*

I didn't like the play, but then I saw it under adverse conditions—the curtain was up.
                    GEORGE S. KAUFMAN

When I saw *Annie* (at a date's insistence) I had to hit myself on the head afterward with a small hammer to get that stupid "Tomorrow" song out of my head. IAN SHOALES

If you will only take the precaution to go in long enough after it commences and to come out long enough before it is over, you will not find it wearisome. GEORGE BERNARD SHAW reviewing Gounod's *Redemption*

Tonstant Weader fwowed up.
DOROTHY PARKER reviewing
The House at Pooh Corner

The affair between Margot Asquith and Margot Asquith will live as one of the prettiest love stories in all history. DOROTHY PARKER reviewing *The Autobiography of Margot Asquith*

Anybody who doesn't like this book is healthy.
GROUCHO MARX on Oscar Levant's
The Memoirs of an Amnesiac

Very nice, but there are dull stretches.
COMTE DE RIVAROL on a two-line poem

This is not a novel to be tossed aside lightly. It should be thrown with great force.

DOROTHY PARKER

I fell asleep reading a dull book, and I dreamed that I was reading on, so I awoke from sheer boredom.

HEINRICH HEINE

Your manuscript is both good and original; but the part that is good is not original, and the part that is original is not good.

SAMUEL JOHNSON

The banging and slamming and booming and crashing [in *Lohengrin*] were something beyond belief. The racking and pitiless pain of it remains stored up in my memory alongside the memory of the time that I had my teeth fixed.

MARK TWAIN

I like Wagner's music better than any other music. It is so loud that one can talk the whole time without people hearing what one says. That is a great advantage.

OSCAR WILDE

Wagner's music is better than it sounds.

MARK TWAIN

Is Wagner actually a man? Is he not rather a disease? Everything he touches falls ill. He has made music sick.

FRIEDRICH WILHELM NIETZSCHE

Leonard Bernstein has been disclosing musical secrets that have been well known for over four hundred years.

OSCAR LEVANT

There are two ways of disliking poetry; one way is to dislike it, the other is to read Pope.

OSCAR WILDE

Seagulls, as the film stresses, subsist on garbage, and, I guess, you are what you eat.

JOHN SIMON reviewing
Jonathan Livingston Seagull

She runs the gamut of emotions from A to B.

DOROTHY PARKER on Katharine Hepburn

I never watch the Dinah Shore show—I'm a diabetic.

OSCAR LEVANT

QUOTES ON "C"

In California everyone goes to a therapist, is a therapist, or is a therapist going to a therapist.

TRUMAN CAPOTE

California, the department store state.

RAYMOND CHANDLER

California: The west coast of Iowa.

JOAN DIDION

The Screwy State.   ROBERT GRAVES

Most people in California came from somewhere else. They moved to California so they could name their kids Rainbow or Mailbox, and purchase tubular Swedish furniture without getting laughed at. It's a tenet also in California that the fiber of your clothing is equivalent to your moral fiber. Your "lifestyle" (as they say) is your ethic. This means that in California you don't really have to do anything, except look healthy, think good thoughts and pat yourself on the back about what a good person you are. And waiters in California want to be called by their first name. I don't know why.   IAN SHOALES

It's a scientific fact that if you stay in California you lose one point of your IQ every year.

TRUMAN CAPOTE

Living in California adds ten years to a man's life.
And those extra ten years I'd like to spend in New
York.   HARRY RUBY

It is the land of perpetual pubescence, where cultural lag is mistaken for renaissance.
                                    ASHLEY MONTAGU

California is a tragic country—like Palestine, like
every Promised Land. CHRISTOPHER ISHERWOOD

A wet dream in the mind of New York.
                                    ERICA JONG

Californians invented the concept of life-style. This
alone warrants their doom.   DON DELILLO

_____ CALMNESS _____

Nothing is so aggravating as calmness.
                                    OSCAR WILDE

_____ CANADA _____

A few acres of snow.   VOLTAIRE

_____ CANADIANS _____

When I was there I found their jokes like their
roads—very long and not very good, leading to a
little tin point of a spire which has been remorselessly obvious for miles without seeming to get
any nearer.   SAMUEL BUTLER

_____ CAPITAL PUNISHMENT _____

There is no satisfaction in hanging a man who
does not object to it.   GEORGE BERNARD SHAW

When I came back to Dublin I was court martialed in my absence and sentenced to death in my absence, so I said they could shoot me in my absence.
BRENDAN BEHAN

CATS

They smell and they snarl and they scratch; they have a singular aptitude for shredding rugs, drapes and upholstery; they're sneaky, selfish and not particularly smart; they are disloyal, condescending and totally useless in any rodent-free environment.
JEAN-MICHEL CHAPEREAU

CELEBRITY

A sign of celebrity is that his name is often worth more than his services.
DANIEL J. BOORSTIN

CHARM

All charming people, I fancy, are spoiled. It is the secret of their attraction.
OSCAR WILDE

CHASTITY

Chastity: the most unnatural of the sexual perversions.
ALDOUS HUXLEY

We may eventually come to realize that chastity is no more a virtue than malnutrition.
ALEX COMFORT

Chastity always takes its toll. In some it produces pimples; in others, sex laws.
KARL KRAUS

One of the serious obstacles to the improvement
of our race is indiscriminate charity.

ANDREW CARNEGIE

Chess is a foolish expedient for making idle people
believe they are doing something very clever when
they are only wasting their time.

GEORGE BERNARD SHAW

As elaborate a waste of human intelligence as you
can find outside an advertising agency.

RAYMOND CHANDLER

Chess is seldom found above the upper-middle
class: it's too hard.   PAUL FUSSELL

This vicious, stinking zoo, this mean-grinning,
mace-smelling boneyard of a city: an elegant
rockpile of a monument to everything cruel and
stupid and corrupt in the human spirit.

HUNTER S. THOMPSON

Childhood, *n.* The period of human life interme-
diate between the idiocy of infancy and the folly
of youth—two removes from the sin of manhood
and three from the remorse of age.

AMBROSE BIERCE

I love children, especially when they cry, for then someone takes them away. NANCY MITFORD

Of children as of procreation—the pleasure momentary, the posture ridiculous, the expense damnable. EVELYN WAUGH

If a child shows himself to be incorrigible, he should be decently and quietly beheaded at the age of twelve, lest he grow to maturity, marry, and perpetuate his kind. DON MARQUIS

Children should neither be seen nor heard from—ever again. W. C. FIELDS

At eight or nine, I suppose, intelligence is no more than a small spot of light on the floor of a large and murky room. H. L. MENCKEN

There are three terrible ages of childhood—1 to 10, 10 to 20, and 20 to 30.

CLEVELAND AMORY

The secret of dealing successfully with a child is not to be its parent. MELL LAZARUS

The best way to keep children at home is to make the home atmosphere pleasant—and let the air out of the tires. DOROTHY PARKER

By the time the youngest children have learned to keep the house tidy, the oldest grandchildren are on hand to tear it to pieces.

CHRISTOPHER MORLEY

I like children. If they're properly cooked.
W. C. FIELDS

Children are never too tender to be whipped. Like tough beefsteaks, the more you beat them, the more tender they become.   EDGAR ALLAN POE

Insanity is hereditary; you can get it from your children.   SAM LEVENSON

My children weary me. I can only see them as defective adults; feckless, destructive, frivolous, sensual, humorless.   EVELYN WAUGH

A son of my own! Oh, no, no, no! Let my flesh perish with me, and let me not transmit to anyone the boredom and the ignominiousness of life.
GUSTAVE FLAUBERT

Go back to reform school, you little nose-picker.
W. C. FIELDS

Contemporary American children, if they are old enough to grasp the concept of Santa Claus by Thanksgiving, are able to see through it by December 15th.   ROY BLOUNT, JR.

When childhood dies, its corpses are called adults and they enter society, one of the politer names of hell. That is why we dread children, even if we love them. They show us the state of our decay.
BRIAN ALDISS

A child is a curly, dimpled lunatic.
RALPH WALDO EMERSON

What is more enchanting than the voices of young
people when you can't hear what they say?
LOGAN PEARSALL SMITH

Children make the most desirable opponents in
Scrabble as they are both easy to beat and fun to
cheat. FRAN LEBOWITZ

We are given children to test us and make us more
spiritual. GEORGE F. WILL

CHRIST

Christ: an anarchist who succeeded. That's all.
ANDRÉ MALRAUX

A parish demagogue. PERCY BYSSHE SHELLEY

Everyone in the world is Christ and they are all
crucified. SHERWOOD ANDERSON

Christ died for our sins. Dare we make his martyrdom meaningless by not committing them?
JULES FEIFFER

If Christ were here now there is one thing he
would not be—a Christian. MARK TWAIN

CHRISTIANITY

Christian, *n*. One who follows the teachings of
Christ insofar as they are not inconsistent with a
life of sin. AMBROSE BIERCE

The last Christian died on the cross.
FRIEDRICH WILHELM NIETZSCHE

I admire the serene assurance of those who have religious faith. It is wonderful to observe the calm confidence of a Christian with four aces.

MARK TWAIN

> I call Christianity the one great curse, the one great intrinsic depravity, the one great instinct of revenge, for which no means are venemous enough, or secret, subterranean and small enough—I call it the one immortal blemish upon the human race.
>
> FRIEDRICH WILHELM NIETZSCHE

What I got in Sunday School . . . was simply a firm conviction that the Christian faith was full of palpable absurdities, and the Christian God preposterous.

H. L. MENCKEN

> Organized Christianity has probably done more to retard the ideals that were its founder's than any other agency in the world.
>
> RICHARD LE GALLIENNE

The Christian religion not only was at first attended with miracles, but even at this day cannot be believed by any reasonable person without one.

DAVID HUME

> People in general are equally horrified at hearing the Christian religion doubted, and at seeing it practiced.
>
> SAMUEL BUTLER

The Christian ideal has not been tried and found wanting; it has been found difficult and left untried.

G. K. CHESTERTON

Going to church doesn't make you a Christian any
more than going to the garage makes you a car.
LAURENCE J. PETER

People may say what they like about the decay of
Christianity; the religious system that produced
green Chartreuse can never really die.   SAKI

―――――――――――― CIVILIZATION ――――――――――――

Civilization is a limitless multiplication of unnecessary necessities.   MARK TWAIN

The end of the human race will be that it will
eventually die of civilization.
RALPH WALDO EMERSON

The civilization of one epoch becomes the manure
of the next.   CYRIL CONNOLLY

The civilized are those who get more out of life
than the uncivilized, and for this the uncivilized
have never forgiven them.   CYRIL CONNOLLY

We are born princes and the civilizing process
makes us frogs.   ERIC BERNE

―――――――――――――― CLASS ――――――――――――――

Each class preaches the importance of those virtues it need not exercise. The rich harp on the
value of thrift, the idle grow eloquent over the
dignity of labor.   OSCAR WILDE

The classes that wash most are those that work
least.   G. K. CHESTERTON

The danger is not that a particular class is unfit to
govern. Every class is unfit to govern.

LORD ACTON

CLERGY

Of learned men, the clergy show the lowest development of professional ethics. Any pastor is free
to cadge customers from the divines of rival sects,
and to denounce the divines themselves as theo-
logical quacks.

H. L. MENCKEN

Clergyman, *n*. A man who undertakes the man-
agement of our spiritual affairs as a method of
bettering his temporal ones.

AMBROSE BIERCE

A clergyman is one who feels himself called upon
to live without working at the expense of the
rascals who work to live.

VOLTAIRE

CLUB

I don't care to belong to a club that accepts people
like me as members.

GROUCHO MARX

COEDS

If all these sweet young things were laid end to
end, I wouldn't be the slightest bit surprised.

DOROTHY PARKER

COLLEGE FOOTBALL

College football would be more interesting if the
faculty played instead of the students—there would

be a great increase in broken arms, legs and necks.
H. L. MENCKEN

————————— COMMON PEOPLE —————————

God must hate the common people, because he made them so common.   PHILIP WYLIE

————————— COMMUNISM —————————

Communism is like one big phone company.
LENNY BRUCE

Communism, like any other revealed religion, is largely made up of prophesies.   H. L. MENCKEN

————————— CONFESSION —————————

Confession is good for the soul only in the sense that a tweed coat is good for dandruff—it is a palliative rather than a remedy.   PETER DE VRIES

Nothing spoils a confession like repentence.
ANATOLE FRANCE

————————— CONGRESS —————————

Congress—these, for the most part, illiterate hacks whose fancy vests are spotted with gravy, and whose speeches, hypocritical, unctuous, and slovenly, are spotted also with the gravy of political patronage.   MARY McCARTHY

It could probably be shown by facts and figures that there is no distinctively native American criminal class except Congress.   MARK TWAIN

Conscience is a mother-in-law whose visit never ends.

H. L. MENCKEN

Conscience and cowardice are really the same things. Conscience is the trade-name of the firm.

OSCAR WILDE

The inner voice which warns us that someone may be looking.

H. L. MENCKEN

CONSERVATIVE

Conservative, *n*. A statesman who is enamored of existing evils, as distinguished from a liberal, who wishes to replace them with others.

AMBROSE BIERCE

CONSISTENCY

Consistency is the last refuge of the unimaginative.

OSCAR WILDE

The only completely consistent people are the dead.

ALDOUS HUXLEY

CONTENTED PEOPLE

I have not a word to say against contented people, so long as they keep quiet. But do not, for goodness sake, let them go strutting about, as they are so fond of doing, crying out that they are the true models for the whole species.

JEROME K. JEROME

Conversation is the enemy of good wine and food.
ALFRED HITCHCOCK

If other people are going to talk, conversation becomes impossible. JAMES McNEILL WHISTLER

A prating barber asked Archelaus how he would be trimmed. He answered, "In silence."
PLUTARCH

During the Samuel Johnson days they had big men enjoying small talk; today we have small men enjoying big talk. FRED ALLEN

The trouble with her is that she lacks the power of conversation but not the power of speech.
GEORGE BERNARD SHAW

CONVICTIONS

Convictions are more dangerous enemies of truth than lies. FRIEDRICH WILHELM NIETZSCHE

CORPORATION

Corporation, *n*. An ingenious device for obtaining individual profit without individual responsibility.
AMBROSE BIERCE

COUNTRY

The country has charms only for those not obliged to stay there. ÉDOUARD MANET

Anybody can be good in the country. There are
no temptations there.   OSCAR WILDE

O Lord! I don't know which is the worst of the
country, the walking or the sitting at home with
nothing to do.   GEORGE BERNARD SHAW

I have no relish for the country; it is a kind of
healthy grave.   SYDNEY SMITH

COURAGE

Courage is the fear of being thought a coward.
                                    HORACE SMITH

CRITICS AND CRITICISM

Critic, *n*. A person who boasts himself hard to
please because nobody tries to please him.
                                    AMBROSE BIERCE

Critics are like eunuchs in a harem: they know
how it's done, they've seen it done every day, but
they're unable to do it themselves.
                                    BRENDAN BEHAN

A critic is a legless man who teaches running.
                                    CHANNING POLLOCK

A critic is a gong at a railroad crossing clanging
loudly and vainly as the train goes by.
                                    CHRISTOPHER MORLEY

Has anybody ever seen a drama critic in the daytime? Of course not. They come out after dark, up
to no good.   P. G. WODEHOUSE

Drooling, driveling, doleful, depressing, dropsical drips.   SIR THOMAS BEECHAM

A book reviewer is usually a barker before the door of a publisher's circus.   AUSTIN O'MALLEY

A dramatic critic is a man who leaves no turn unstoned.   GEORGE BERNARD SHAW

For critics I care the five hundred thousandth part of the tythe of a half-farthing.   CHARLES LAMB

Critics are a dissembling, dishonest, contemptible race of men. Asking a working writer what he thinks about critics is like asking a lamppost what it feels about dogs.   JOHN OSBORNE

I had another dream the other day about music critics. They were small and rodent-like with padlocked ears, as if they had stepped out of a painting by Goya.   IGOR STRAVINSKY

There be some men are born only to suck out the poison of books.   BEN JONSON

Criticism is prejudice made plausible.
               H. L. MENCKEN

Criticism is a study by which men grow important and formidable at very small expense.
               SAMUEL JOHNSON

Criticism is the art wherewith a critic tries to guess himself into a share of the artist's fame.

GEORGE JEAN NATHAN

Reviewing has one advantage over suicide: in suicide you take it out of yourself; in reviewing you take it out of other people.

GEORGE BERNARD SHAW

—————————————— CULT ——————————————

A cult is a religion with no political power.

TOM WOLFE

—————————————— CULTURE ——————————————

Culture is an instrument wielded by professors to manufacture professors, who when their turn comes, will manufacture professors. SIMONE WEIL

—————————————— CURE ——————————————

I have a perfect cure for a sore throat: cut it.

ALFRED HITCHCOCK

—————————————— CYNIC ——————————————

A cynic is a man who, when he smells flowers, looks around for a coffin. H. L. MENCKEN

Cynic, *n*. A blackguard whose faulty vision sees things as they are, not as they ought to be.

AMBROSE BIERCE

A cynic is not merely one who reads bitter lessons from the past, he is one who is prematurely disappointed in the future. SIDNEY HARRIS

What is a cynic? A man who knows the price of everything and the value of nothing.

OSCAR WILDE

CYNICISM

Cynicism is an unpleasant way of saying the truth.

LILLIAN HELLMAN

The power of accurate observation is commonly called cynicism by those who have not got it.

GEORGE BERNARD SHAW

CALVIN TRILLIN

Sausage-Eating, Slothful Sweetheart

CALVIN TRILLIN was born and raised in Kansas City. He graduated from Yale in 1957, did a hitch in the Army, and then joined
Time magazine. In 1963, he became a staff writer for *The New
Yorker* where, from 1967 to 1982, he wrote a series of articles
called "U.S. Journal." He wrote a column for *The Nation* from
1978 to 1985, which he subsequently collected in two books:
Uncivil Liberties and *With All Disrespect*. He has published two

novels and a trio of books on eating and writes a nationally syndicated newspaper column, *Uncivil Liberties*. He lives in New York with his wife, Alice, and their two daughters.

JW: *Your wife has called you a "sausage-eating, slothful crank."*
CT: She has. But she also says that down deep I'm really a sweetheart.
JW: *A sweetheart, not a curmudgeon?*
CT: I've been accused of being amiable. Good-humored is another accusation that's been made against me.
JW: *Then you don't regard yourself as a curmudgeon?*
CT: Certainly not. I consider myself a good-natured, sweet-hearted person.
JW: *Would you at least say that you have the habit of pointing out unpleasant facts?*
CT: Yes, in an amiable way. But I think that's true of not only people who comment on things but it's generally true of reporters, because most people don't remember things the way they happen.
JW: *You've suggested that the advance for a book should be at least as much as the cost of the lunch over which it was discussed. Have you received proper recognition for this contribution?*
CT: Nobody's ever paid attention to any of my laws. The one about advances was just one of a number of suggestions about the publishing industry. The average trade book has a shelf life of between milk and yogurt, except for books by any member of the Irving Wallace family—they have preservatives. That was sup-

posed to be a New York City ordinance because most of the publishing industry is in New York. I suggested that any novel that weighs over three pounds or deals with more than four generations of the same family should be required to have in the front matter the names of the characters, the page on which they're introduced, their nicknames or pet names, and their sexual proclivities. Nobody took that seriously. After the Watergate books, I suggested that an author who had committed a felony while on the public payroll should be required to donate the royalties to a scholarship fund to send Gypsies to the Harvard Business School. None of these things have ever been taken seriously.

JW: *You've also propounded a number of federal laws.*

CT: Yes, anybody caught selling macramé in public should be dyed a natural color and hung out to dry. Citizen's arrest for mime. I've never had any of my laws passed or even discussed.

JW: *Have you tried lobbying your congressman?*

CT: I don't know who my congressman is. We don't have a congressman anymore in the Village. We used to have a congressman, but they took him away. Then for a while we had a congressman who supposedly was the congressman from Staten Island, but the *Village Voice,* all during the "Koreagate" scandal, referred to him as "Democrat, Seoul."

JW: *Your first book came out in 1964. Have you been satisfied with the way your books have been handled by your various publishers?*

CT: For a while I was what I call an "itinerant loss-leader." I went from publisher to publisher, and if someone said to them, "You just put out things that are going to make a lot of money," they could say, "No, we publish Trillin and he never earns his advance back."

JW: *Are there problems in writing satire?*

CT: I think there are two problems: The first, of course, is that people take it seriously. The second is that what happens in America is so bizarre, what you write might turn out to be serious compared to what has just happened. That's what I call the Harry Golden Rule, which is named after the late Harry Golden, who used to publish *The Carolina Israelite.* During the fifties Harry Golden observed that white people in his part of North Carolina didn't mind standing up with black people, they only minded sitting down with them, so he suggested that the way to integrate the schools was to simply take the chairs out and have the kids stand up at their desks. I think he called it, "Harry Golden's Plan for the Vertical Integration of the Schools." About a year later some library was ordered integrated by a federal court and it proceeded to take the chairs out. This is what is called, "being blindsided by the truth," which is a real problem in America. The Harry Golden Rule, properly stated, is that in present-day America it's very difficult, when commenting on events of the day, to invent something so bizarre that it might not actually come to pass while your piece is still on the presses. Certainly *The Nation* readership used to take my stuff too seriously. Occasionally they would write letters like, "Trillin is usually boring or offensive and this week he's both."

JW: *Do you think the misunderstanding of satire has anything to do with poor reading skills?*

CT: No, I think it has to do with just a lack of a sense of humor. Sometimes, of course, *we're* at fault. Sometimes it's not clear what's real and what isn't because we didn't set it up right.

JW: *Do you mind doing book tours?*

CT: No, but I have some doubt about how much good they do. You wonder about these people who watch television at four-thirty in the afternoon to see various recipes and people play the saw. Why aren't they reading? It's obvious that touring helps books like *How to Remove Your Own Appendix by Thinking You're the Real You,* because they're not actually books. But books that require *reading,* I'm not so sure.

JW: *Do you like California?*

CT: There's a theory that almost anything that's fun is going to be ruined sooner or later by people from California. They tend to bring seriousness to subjects that don't deserve it, and they tend to get very good at things that weren't very important in the first place. The example I use is coming across somebody on Venice Beach who had perfected bubble blowing—knew everything about it, produced these huge bubbles, and spoke at length at the tiniest opportunity about what went into a bubble.

JW: *Have you taken a position on religious fundamentalism?*

CT: I just wrote a column expressing disappointment that one of my phrases hasn't found its way into the political lexicon in this country. The phrase is *deity overload,* the theory that God may be all-powerful and all-knowing but that He is not all-patient. He's got a lot on his plate, and at some point He may look down with disfavor when Pat Robertson asks His blessing for a deal to trade his delegates for the vice presidential nomination.

JW: *You've spent vacations in France. Have you had good relations with the French?*

CT: One of the problems that Americans have with the French is that Americans think, before they go to France, that French people are basically like Maurice Chevalier. That's their model of French people, and in fact, there was only one Maurice Chevalier and he lived in California. So they go to France expecting to hear someone say, "Sank heaven for leetle girls," and instead they find some really sullen bureaucrat saying, "Grandmoser's maiden name?" and they get irritated. On the other hand, when Americans go to Italy, where a lot of people are still Ezio Pinza, it makes them feel better.

JW: *I notice you have cats.*

CT: Yes, but I wish we didn't have any cats. I have nothing against them other than the fact that they're useless and destructive and a pain in the ass. Nothing at all. I'm not prejudiced against cats, but these two happen to be particularly dreadful cats, even as cats. They're also noisy cats. They're Siamese and they shout.

JW: *Let me ask you about some modern annoyances. How about blow-in cards, those subscription form things that fall out of magazines?*

CT: I hardly notice them, probably because I read so many magazines on airplanes.

JW: *How about perfumed perfume ads?*

CT: I truly hate them. I don't think they should be allowed. It is not a constitutionally protected form of expression; there's nothing in the First Amendment about freedom to stink. That's basically my theory on mime: They've obviously waived their First Amendment rights by refusing to speak.

JW: *Do you have problems with car alarms?*

CT: We do, at least on Saturday nights, when the Village becomes what we sometimes call "Jerseyated." It's a wonderful time to rob houses in Ridgefield. They're constantly going off around here. I think there should be a definite rule about car alarms: You should have the right to break the window and turn it off.

JW: *Do you run?*

CT: No. I suppose the odd jogger looks normal, but runners, people who actually run in marathons, just look pathetic to me. It can't be worth it. They look like those people in the health-food store: gray pallor, stringy little beards, sunken chests. They make you want to call 911.

QUOTES ON "D"

I knew her before she was a virgin.

OSCAR LEVANT

DEATH

It's not that I'm afraid to die. I just don't want to be there when it happens.
WOODY ALLEN

Sleep is lovely, death is better still, not to have been born is of course the miracle.
HEINRICH HEINE

Those who welcome death have only tried it from the ears up.
WILSON MIZNER

DEBT

A man properly must pay the fiddler. In my case it so happened that a whole symphony orchestra had to be subsidized.
JOHN BARRYMORE

DECENCY

Decency . . . must be an even more exhausting state to maintain than its opposite. Those who succeed seem to need a stupefying amount of sleep.
QUENTIN CRISP

DELUSION

The final delusion is the belief that one has lost all delusions.
MAURICE CHAPELAIN

A democracy is a government in the hands of men of
low birth, no property, and vulgar employments.
ARISTOTLE

Democracy encourages the majority to decide things
about which the majority is blissfully ignorant.
JOHN SIMON

The substitution of election by the incompetent
many for appointment by the corrupt few.
GEORGE BERNARD SHAW

The bludgeoning of the people, by the people, for
the people. OSCAR WILDE

Democracy is a process by which the people are
free to choose the man who will get the blame.
LAURENCE J. PETER

The worship of jackals by jackasses.
H. L. MENCKEN

Democracy becomes a government of bullies, tem-
pered by editors. RALPH WALDO EMERSON

Democracy gives every man the right to be his
own oppressor. JAMES RUSSELL LOWELL

An aristocracy of blackguards. LORD BYRON

In every well-governed state wealth is a sacred
thing; in democracies it is the only sacred thing.
ANATOLE FRANCE

DIAGNOSIS

One of the most common of all diseases is diagnosis.
KARL KRAUS

DIARY

Keep a diary and one day it'll keep you.
MAE WEST

DINNER THEATER

"Dinner theater," a way of positively guaranteeing that both food and theater will be amateur and mediocre, which means unthreatening and therefore desirable. PAUL FUSSELL

DIPLOMACY

The patriotic art of lying for one's country.
AMBROSE BIERCE

The principle of give and take is the principle of diplomacy— give one and take ten.
MARK TWAIN

I'm convinced there's a small room in the attic of the Foreign Office where future diplomats are taught to stammer. PETER USTINOV

DISHONESTY

There's one way to find out if a man is honest: ask him; if he says yes, you know he is crooked.
MARK TWAIN

We have to distrust each other. It's our only defense against betrayal.   TENNESSEE WILLIAMS

Joyous distrust is a sign of health. Everything absolute belongs to pathology.
FRIEDRICH WILHELM NIETZSCHE

———————————————————— DOCTORS ————————————————————

A doctor's reputation is made by the number of eminent men who die under his care.
GEORGE BERNARD SHAW

God heals, and the doctor takes the fee.
BENJAMIN FRANKLIN

The best doctor is the one you run for and can't find.   DENIS DIDEROT

Doctors are men who prescribe medicines of which they know little, to cure diseases of which they know less, in human beings of whom they know nothing.   VOLTAIRE

The art of medicine consists in amusing the patient while nature cures the disease.   VOLTAIRE

Doctors are just the same as lawyers; the only difference is that lawyers merely rob you, whereas doctors rob you and kill you, too.
ANTON CHEKHOV

The greatest pleasure of a dog is that you may make a fool of yourself with him, and not only will he not scold you, but he will make a fool of himself too.   SAMUEL BUTLER

Histories are more full of examples of the fidelity of dogs than of friends.   ALEXANDER POPE

The average dog is a nicer person than the average person.   ANDREW A. ROONEY

If you pick up a starving dog and make him prosperous, he will not bite you. This is the principal difference between a dog and a man.

MARK TWAIN

The dog has seldom been successful in pulling man up to its level of sagacity, but man has frequently dragged the dog down to his.

JAMES THURBER

To be sure, the dog is loyal. But why, on that account, should we take him as an example? He is loyal to men, not to other dogs.   KARL KRAUS

Has he bit any of the children yet? If he has, have them shot, and keep him for curiosity, to see if it was the hydrophobia.   CHARLES LAMB

_____ DOG OWNERS _____

To his dog, every man is Napoleon; hence the constant popularity of dogs.   ALDOUS HUXLEY

I loathe people who keep dogs. They are cowards
who haven't got the guts to bite people themselves.
AUGUST STRINDBERG

_____ DRINKING _____

Drinking makes such fools of people, and people
are such fools to begin with that it's compounding
a felony. ROBERT BENCHLEY

I envy people who drink—at least they know what
to blame everything on. OSCAR LEVANT

I only drink to make other people seem interesting.
GEORGE JEAN NATHAN

Alcohol is a very necessary article. It enables Parliament to do things at eleven at night that no
sane person would do at eleven in the morning.
GEORGE BERNARD SHAW

I have taken more out of alcohol than alcohol has
taken out of me. WINSTON CHURCHILL

So who's in a hurry?
ROBERT BENCHLEY in response to a warning that
drinking is "slow poison."

_____ DUTY _____

When a stupid man is doing something he is
ashamed of, he always declares that it is his duty.
GEORGE BERNARD SHAW

Duty, *n*. That which sternly impels us in the direction of profit, along the line of desire.
AMBROSE BIERCE

QUOTES ON "E"

If all economists were laid end to end, they would not reach a conclusion. GEORGE BERNARD SHAW

EDITOR

An editor should have a pimp for a brother, so he'd have someone to look up to. GENE FOWLER

EDUCATION

Education: the inculcation of the incomprehensible into the indifferent by the incompetent.
JOHN MAYNARD KEYNES

Education, *n*. That which discloses to the wise and disguises from the foolish their lack of understanding. AMBROSE BIERCE

Soap and education are not as sudden as a massacre but they are more deadly in the long run.
MARK TWAIN

Men are born ignorant, not stupid; they are made stupid by education. BERTRAND RUSSELL

Education is a state-controlled manufactory of echoes. NORMAN DOUGLAS

We are shut up in schools and college recitation rooms for ten or fifteen years, and come out at last with a bellyful of words and do not know a thing.
RALPH WALDO EMERSON

Society produces rogues, and education makes one
rogue cleverer than another.   OSCAR WILDE

> Education is a method whereby one acquires a
> higher grade of prejudices.   LAURENCE J. PETER

I prefer the company of peasants because they
have not been educated sufficiently to reason
incorrectly.   MICHEL DE MONTAIGNE

> How is it that little children are so intelligent and
> men so stupid? It must be education that does it.
> ALEXANDRE DUMAS *fils*

You can't expect a boy to be depraved until he has
been to a good school.   SAKI

> "Whom are you?" said he, for he had been to
> night school.   GEORGE ADE

ENEMIES

One should forgive one's enemies, but not before
they are hanged.   HEINRICH HEINE

ENGLAND AND THE ENGLISH

> England is the most class-ridden country under
> the sun. It is a land of snobbery and privilege,
> ruled largely by the old and silly.
> GEORGE ORWELL

There is such a thing as too much couth.
S. J. PERELMAN

England has forty-two religions and only two sauces. VOLTAIRE

The English never smash in a face. They merely refrain from asking it to dinner.

MARGARET HALSEY

The English instinctively admire any man who has no talent and is modest about it.

JAMES AGATE

The English think incompetence is the same thing as sincerity. QUENTIN CRISP

Curse the blasted jelly-boned swines, the slimy belly-wriggling invertebrates, the miserable sodding rotters, the flaming sods, the sniveling, dribbling, dithering, palsied pulseless lot that make up England today. They've got white of egg in their veins, and their spunk is that watery it's a marvel they can breed . . . Why, why, why, was I born an Englishman! D. H. LAWRENCE

——————————— EQUALITY ———————————

Equality may perhaps be a right, but no power on earth can ever turn it into a fact.

HONORÉ DE BALZAC

That all men are created equal is a proposition to which, at ordinary times, no sane individual has ever given his assent. ALDOUS HUXLEY

——————————— ETHICS ———————————

Grub first, then ethics. BERTOLT BRECHT

Exercise is bunk. If you are healthy, you don't
need it; if you are sick, you shouldn't take it.
HENRY FORD

I believe every human has a finite number of heart-
beats. I don't intend to waste any of mine running
around doing exercises.   NEIL ARMSTRONG

_____ EXISTENCE _____

The very purpose of existence is to reconcile the
glowing opinion we hold of ourselves with the
appalling things that other people think about us.
QUENTIN CRISP

_____ EXISTENTIALISM _____

Existentialism means that no one else can take a
bath for you.   DELMORE SCHWARTZ

_____ EXPERIENCE _____

Experience is the name everyone gives to their
mistakes.   OSCAR WILDE

Experience, *n*. The wisdom that enables us to
recognize as an undesirable old acquaintance the
folly that we have already embraced.
AMBROSE BIERCE

We learn from experience that men never learn
anything from experience.

GEORGE BERNARD SHAW

W. C. FIELDS

A Definite Personality

WILLIAM CLAUDE DUKENFIELD was born in Philadelphia in 1880 and was raised above the saloon where his father tended bar. His mother was a strong woman, bitter about her lot in life, and he probably inherited his wisecracking, side-of-the-mouth style from her: She would sit on the porch with her young son and entertain him with a snide, running commentary about passing neighbors.

Contrary to legend, he didn't run away from home after a fight with his father but left under amicable circumstances at the age of eleven to earn his fortune in show business. He was inspired by vaudeville performers of the day and he discovered early on what he described as his "fatal facility" for juggling. He taught himself juggling routines and developed brilliant sight gags involving hats, golf clubs, and pool cues through long hours of practice and eventually earned a reputation as a disciplined professional.

He lost his illusions early; after being cheated by unscrupulous booking agents and crooked theater managers, he never again felt financially secure. At the height of his movie career, when he was earning $100,000 a picture, he regularly deposited money in banks all over the country under fictitious names. Since he never revealed the account numbers to anyone, and since no bank records were found among his possessions, the money was never recovered by his heirs.

He married a showgirl named Harriet Hughes in 1900. They lived together for seven years and produced a son, then separated, never to reconcile. He subordinated his family, his social life, and ultimately his happiness to the demands of his career and turned his personal tragedies into comedy: The characters in his pictures usually include a bratty son, a shrewish wife, a domineering mother-in-law, and a loving daughter (the daughter he never had).

He was naturally undemonstrative and easily hurt, so he affected a phony manorial demeanor to conceal his vulnerability.

He once told an interviewer that he decided at an early age to become "a definite personality." He strove to be a part of the world but was an outcast. According to Louise Brooks, the former ingenue who wrote perceptively about the Hollywood of the twenties and thirties, Fields "stretched out his hand to Beauty and Love and they thrust it away."

Even his legendary drinking was an outgrowth of his loneliness: He secured the companionship of his fellow vaudeville performers with free whiskey, even though he was himself a teetotaler (as a juggler he didn't want to hurt his timing). But once he learned how to drink, he would consume at least a quart of gin a day for the rest of his life.

He played himself in most of his pictures (with the exception of Micawber in *David Copperfield*). He played lovable rogues, bumbling dipsomaniacs, harassed family men plagued by domineering wives and mothers-in-law. He wrote all his pictures under assumed names—Mahatma Kane Jeeves, Charles Bogle, Otis Criblecoblis—but seemed incapable of delivering the lines as written.

Fields died on Christmas Day in 1946. Contrary to legend, he isn't buried in Philadelphia; his ashes are in an unmarked urn at Forest Lawn in Hollywood. During his last illness he was confined to a hospital bed, and a visitor was shocked to catch him reading the Bible. "Just looking for loopholes," he explained.

A FLAGON OF FIELDS

Once, during Prohibition, I was forced to live for days on nothing but food and water.

A woman drove me to drink, and I never even had the courtesy to thank her.

I always keep a supply of stimulant handy in case I see a snake, which I also keep handy.

What contemptible scoundrel stole the cork from my lunch?

My illness is due to my doctor's insistence that I drink milk, a whitish fluid they force down helpless babies.

The cost of living has gone up another dollar a quart.

I exercise self-control and never touch any beverage stronger than gin before breakfast.

Anybody who hates dogs and loves whiskey can't be all bad.

QUOTES ON "F"

_____ FAILURE _____

No one is completely unhappy at the failure of his
best friend.   GROUCHO MARX

_____ FAITH _____

Faith, *n.* Belief without evidence in what is told by
one who speaks without knowledge, of things without parallel. `   AMBROSE BIERCE

Faith may be defined briefly as an illogical belief
in the occurrence of the improbable.
                                        H. L. MENCKEN

A casual stroll through the lunatic asylum shows
that faith does not prove anything.
                          FRIEDRICH WILHELM NIETZSCHE

The most common of all follies is to believe pas-
sionately in the palpably not true. It is the chief
occupation of mankind.   H. L. MENCKEN

_____ FAME _____

Fame is a vapor; popularity an accident; the only
earthly certainty is oblivion.   MARK TWAIN

_____ FAMILY _____

When I can do no longer bear to think of the
victims of broken homes, I begin to think of the
victims of intact ones.   PETER DE VRIES

Sacred family! . . . The supposed home of all the
virtues, where innocent children are tortured into
their first falsehoods, where wills are broken by
parental tyranny, and self-respect is smothered by
crowded, jostling egos.   AUGUST STRINDBERG

The family is a court of justice which never shuts
down for night or day.   MALCOLM DE CHAZAL

The family is the ultimate American fascism.
PAUL GOODMAN

A family is but too often a commonwealth of
malignants.   ALEXANDER POPE

A married man with a family will do anything for
money.   CHARLES DE TALLEYRAND

Having a family is like having a bowling alley
installed in your brain.   MARTIN MULL

Home life as we understand it is no more natural
to us than a cage is natural to a cockatoo.
GEORGE BERNARD SHAW

—————————— FARM ——————————

A farm is an irregular patch of nettles bounded by
short-term notes, containing a fool and his wife
who didn't know enough to stay in the city.
S. J. PERELMAN

—————————— FASHION ——————————

Never despise fashion. It's what we have instead
of God.   MALCOLM BRADBURY

Fashion is a form of ugliness so intolerable that we have to alter it every six months.

OSCAR WILDE

Fashions are the only induced epidemics, proving that epidemics can be induced by tradesmen.

GEORGE BERNARD SHAW

FAST FOOD

We were taken to a fast-food café where our order was fed into a computer. Our hamburgers, made from the flesh of chemically impregnated cattle, had been broiled over counterfeit charcoal, placed between slices of artifically flavored cardboard and served to us by recycled juvenile delinquents.

JEAN-MICHEL CHAPEREAU

Scrambled eggs should never be assembled in vat-sized proportions. ROY BLOUNT, JR.

FATHER

I grew up to have my father's looks—my father's speech patterns—my father's posture—my father's walk—my father's opinions and my mother's contempt for my father. JULES FEIFFER

FAVORITES

Favorite animal: steak. FRAN LEBOWITZ

Favorite color: I hate colors. IAN SHOALES

FEMINISTS

I don't understand guys who call themselves feminist. That's like the time Hubert Humphrey, running for President, told a black audience he was a soul brother. ROY BLOUNT, JR.

FILM

If my film makes one more person miserable, I've done my job. WOODY ALLEN

FINANCE

Finance is the art of passing currency from hand to hand until it finally disappears.
ROBERT W. SARNOFF

FISHING

Fishing is a delusion entirely surrounded by liars in old clothes. DON MARQUIS

Fishing, with me, has always been an excuse to drink in the daytime. JIMMY CANNON

FISHING ROD

A fishing rod is a stick with a hook at one end and a fool at the other. SAMUEL JOHNSON

FLATTERY

I hate careless flattery, the kind that exhausts you in your effort to believe it. WILSON MIZNER

FOOD

Do you know on this one block you can buy croissants in five different places? There's one store

called Bonjour Croissant. It makes me want to go
to Paris and open a store called Hello Toast.

FRAN LEBOWITZ

FORGIVENESS

Always forgive your enemies—nothing annoys them
so much.

OSCAR WILDE

FORK

Fork, *n*. An instrument used chiefly for the purpose of putting dead animals into the mouth.

AMBROSE BIERCE

FRANCE AND THE FRENCH

A relatively small and eternally quarrelsome country in Western Europe, fountainhead of rationalist
political manias, militarily impotent, historically
inglorious during the past century, democratically
bankrupt, Communist-infiltrated from top to
bottom.

WILLIAM F. BUCKLEY, JR.

France is the only country where the money falls
apart and you can't tear the toilet paper.

BILLY WILDER

What I gained by being in France was learning to
be better satisfied with my own country.

SAMUEL JOHNSON

I would have loved it—without the French.

D. H. LAWRENCE

Everything is on such a clear financial basis in France. It is the simplest country to live in. No one makes things complicated by becoming your friend for any obscure reason. If you want people to like you, you have only to spend a little money.

ERNEST HEMINGWAY

Frenchmen are like gunpowder, each by itself smutty and contemptible, but mass them together and they are terrible indeed!

SAMUEL TAYLOR COLERIDGE

The French probably invented the very notion of discretion. It's not that they feel that what you don't know won't hurt you; they feel that what you don't know won't hurt them. To the French lying is simply talking.

FRAN LEBOWITZ

They aren't much at fighting wars anymore. Despite their reputation for fashion, their women have spindly legs. Their music is sappy. But they do know how to whip up a plate of grub.

MIKE ROYKO

Every Frenchman wants to enjoy one or more privileges; that's the way he shows his passion for equality.

CHARLES DE GAULLE

Germans with good food.

FRAN LEBOWITZ

—————————— FREEDOM ——————————

When people are free to do as they please, they usually imitate each other.

ERIC HOFFER

The only man who is really free is the one who can turn down an invitation to dinner without giving any excuse.   JULES RENARD

You are free and that is why you are lost.
                                                    FRANZ KAFKA

————————— FREEDOM OF THE PRESS —————————

Freedom of the press is limited to those who own one.   A. J. LIEBLING

————————————— FREE LUNCH —————————————

There is no free lunch.   MILTON FRIEDMAN

————————————— FRENCH FRIES —————————————

The French fried potato has become an inescapable horror in almost every public eating place in the country. "French fries," say the menus, but they are not French fries any longer. They are a furry-textured substance with the taste of plastic wood.   RUSSELL BAKER

————————————— FREUD, SIGMUND —————————————

I think he's crude, I think he's medieval, and I don't want an elderly gentleman from Vienna with an umbrella inflicting his dreams upon me.
                                                    VLADIMIR NABOKOV

Sigmund Freud was a half-baked Viennese quack. Our literature, culture, and the films of Woody Allen would be better today if Freud had never written a word.   IAN SHOALES

Think twice before you speak to a friend in need.
AMBROSE BIERCE

When one is trying to do something beyond his known powers it is useless to seek the approval of friends. Friends are at their best in moments of defeat.
HENRY MILLER

May God defend me from my friends: I can defend myself from my enemies.
VOLTAIRE

It takes your enemy and your friend, working together, to hurt you: the one to slander you, and the other to bring the news to you.
MARK TWAIN

Every time a friend succeeds, I die a little.
GORE VIDAL

The one thing your friends will never forgive you is your happiness.
ALBERT CAMUS

It is well, when judging a friend, to remember that he is judging you with the same godlike and superior impartiality.
ARNOLD BENNETT

A friend who is very near and dear may in time become as useless as a relative.
GEORGE ADE

When a man takes to his bed, nearly all his friends have a secret desire to see him die; some to prove that his health is inferior to their own, others in the disinterested hope of being able to study a death agony.
CHARLES BAUDELAIRE

We cherish our friends not for their ability to
amuse us, but for ours to amuse them.
                                    EVELYN WAUGH

Nothing so fortifies a friendship as a belief on the
part of one friend that he is superior to the other.
                                    HONORÉ DE BALZAC

Friendship is a common belief in the same fallacies, mountebanks and hobgoblins.
                                    H. L. MENCKEN

Friendship is a very taxing and arduous form of
leisure activity.   MORTIMER ADLER

————————————— FUNERAL —————————————

I did not attend his funeral, but I wrote a nice
letter saying I approved it.   MARK TWAIN

What bereaved people need is little comic relief,
and this is why funerals are so farcical.
                                    GEORGE BERNARD SHAW

————————————— FUTURE —————————————

The trouble with our times is that the future is not
what it used to be.   PAUL VALÉRY

Only one more indispensable massacre of Capital-
ists or Communists or Fascists or Christians or
Heretics, and there we are in the Golden Future.
                                    ALDOUS HUXLEY

If you want a picture of the future, imagine a boot
stomping on a human face—forever.
                                    GEORGE ORWELL

GEORGE S. KAUFMAN

The Wittiest Man in America

GEORGE S. KAUFMAN was one of the most successful and prolific playwrights in the history of Broadway and one of America's greatest wits. He was born George Kaufman on November 16, 1889, in Pittsburgh to German-Jewish parents. He was raised by a neurotic mother who had lost her first child and was determined to protect George from "germs" by preparing all his food in sterile conditions and preventing him from going outdoors. The pampering instilled in him a lifelong fear of disease and death.

He was a skinny, unathletic, bespectacled kid who responded to the bullying of his schoolmates with quips instead of fists. He wrote stories and poems for his high-school paper and at the age of fourteen collaborated on a play with another boy. He was a devoted reader of "The Conning Tower," Franklin P. Adams's column in the New York *Evening Mail,* and by the age of fifteen he had become a regular contributor under the byline "G. S. K." (Kaufman added the middle initial for euphony.)

His father wanted him to be a lawyer, but George was stricken with pleurisy during his first year of college. The doctor prescribed an outdoor job to hasten his recovery, so George was apprenticed to a land surveyor. By his own account he was an inept surveyor and no lover of the outdoors and was delighted when Adams recommended him for a job writing a humor column at the Washington *Times.* But within a year he was unemployed: One day he was at his desk at the *Times* when the owner, the newspaper mogul Frank Munsey, walked in, took one look at Kaufman, and bellowed, "What's that Jew doing in my city room?" Adams eventually got him a job on the New York *Evening Mail* as a staff writer. He moved from there to the New York *Tribune,* where he began writing theater criticism, and within a few years he became drama editor at *The New York Times.*

In 1917, at the age of twenty-eight, he married Beatrice Bakrow, the daughter of a wealthy Rochester, New York, clothing manufacturer. After their first child was stillborn, they realized they were sexually incompatible and agreed to an "arrangement" whereby each was free to have extramarital affairs but remained devoted to each other in every other way. He was devastated by her sudden death in 1945.

Kaufman's first attempt as a professional playwright was a rewrite of *Someone in the House,* a 1918 play by Larry Evans and Walter Percival. It was a box office disaster on its own, but a flu epidemic didn't help, which prompted Kaufman to write an ad for the show:

> BEWARE OF FLU
> AVOID CROWDS
> SEE "SOMEONE IN THE HOUSE"

He collaborated with Marc Connelly on three plays, beginning with *Dulcy* in 1921. He went on to work with Moss Hart, Edna Ferber, Ring Lardner, Abe Burrows, Herman Mankiewicz, and Howard Dietz. Kaufman's many stage hits included *The Butter and Egg Man, The Solid Gold Cadillac,* and *The Man Who Came to Dinner.* He won two Pulitzer Prizes—for *Of Thee I Sing,* the first musical to win a Pulitzer Prize, and *You Can't Take It With You.* He cowrote, (with Morrie Ryskind) *Animal Crackers, The Cocoanuts,* and *A Night at the Opera* for the Marx Brothers.

Kaufman was tall and lanky, with a prominent nose and thick hair combed into a high pompadour. He was excruciatingly shy: Many of his friends and collaborators described his habit of avoiding eye contact by bending down to pick up imaginary pieces of lint from the carpet. He had a cleanliness compulsion, abhorred outward displays of affection, and hated physical contact except, presumably, with his many sexual conquests (the Broadway producer Max Gordon called him a "male nymphomaniac," and he had a brief affair with Mary Astor which erupted into scandal when her estranged husband published her diary in which she described Kaufman's sexual prowess).

He was an insomniac, a hypochondriac, and a pathologically fussy eater: Though he regularly dined in the finest restaurants, he ordered simple food and avoided sauces because he could not be sure of their ingredients.

Kaufman was a soft-spoken, self-deprecating pessimist who was plagued by self-doubt in spite of repeated success. He was insecure about the value of his work and was convinced that each hit would be his last. He thought himself an impostor who would be found out when the current play finally opened. He was usually wrong. His only real deficiency as a playwright was his reticence about love scenes; he categorically refused to write them, abdicating the responsibility to his collaborators.

His professional generosity was demonstrated in a curtain speech he delivered following the opening of *Once in a Lifetime* (which he wrote with Moss Hart): "I would like the audience to know that eighty percent of this play is Moss Hart." It was probably the other way around, since *Once in a Lifetime* was Hart's first play, and Hart tried to set the record straight in his own curtain speech. Kaufman habitually minimized his own importance in his many collaborative efforts and often refused credit and compensation for his contributions as a playwright, play doctor, and director.

Kaufman was generally polite and considerate, but he had a maniacal hatred for cabdrivers and waiters. He was in a constant state of war with them throughout his adult life. He insisted that waiters took training in ways to exasperate customers, and he treated them accordingly. His mock epitaph for a departed waiter: "God finally caught his eye."

He seldom used four-letter words but could be caustic when provoked by insincerity or stupidity: He once said to a female acquaintance, "You're a birdbrain, and I mean that as an insult to birds." He was not a raconteur but a conversational guerrilla fighter. He would retreat within himself and appear bored and distracted, all the while listening intensely, waiting for the right moment to get off a devastating line.

His dour persona was a fraud. He actually liked people and was generous and compassionate. He cultivated a reputation for penuriousness but was really a soft touch who lent money on the condition the borrower keep quiet about it lest Kaufman's "reputation" be ruined. When Hitler came to power in 1933, he financed the evacuation from Germany of scores of Jews, stood as their financial sponsor when they arrived in the United States, and actually supported many of them until they were settled.

During the late fifties he suffered a series of strokes that left him partially paralyzed and blind in one eye. Toward the end of his life he seemed to have come to terms with his fear of death. He died on June 2, 1961.

Moss Hart eulogized him as follows: "The paradox of his nature was that he felt deeply, yet he sheered from any display of emotion. Almost always, it remained unexpressed."

GEORGE S. KAUFMAN ANECDOTES

At the age of four, his mother told him that an aunt was coming to visit and asked, "It wouldn't hurt to be nice to her, would it?" to which he replied, "That depends on your threshold of pain."

When asked at nine P.M. what he was doing for dinner that evening, he replied, "Digesting it."

During dinner at the Colony, Harpo Marx asked if there was anything you could get there for fifty cents. "Sure," Kaufman answered, "a quarter."

He was piqued by the Marx Brothers' habit of changing his lines. During rehearsals for *Animal Crackers,* Kaufman walked on the stage in mock exasperation and said, "Excuse me for interrupting, but I thought for a minute I actually heard a line I wrote."

At a dinner party he was seated next to a woman who monopolized the conversation all through the meal. By the time the coffee was served, Kaufman could no longer restrain himself. "Madam," he asked, "don't you have any unexpressed thoughts?"

He attended a farewell party in Hollywood for S. N. Behrman, who had just finished writing a screenplay and was returning to New York. Several days later Kaufman ran into Behrman, who had delayed his departure to work on additional dialogue. Kaufman greeted him with, "Ah, forgotten but not gone."

Kaufman was a bridge fanatic who did not suffer incompetent players gladly. When one particularly inept partner asked to be excused to go to the men's room, Kaufman replied, "Gladly—for the first time today I'll know what you have in your hand."

He was partnered with Herman Mankiewicz in a bridge game, and when Mankiewicz made a spectacular blunder, Kaufman exploded. "I know you learned the game this afternoon," he said, "but what *time* this afternoon?"

Another bridge partner, sensing that Kaufman was not pleased with his conduct of the previous hand, asked defensively, "Well, George, how would *you* have played the hand?"

"Under an assumed name," Kaufman shot back.

During a performance of a very bad play, Kaufman leaned forward and politely asked the lady in front of him if she would mind putting on her hat.

William Gaxton, the star of *Of Thee I Sing,* began to get bored with the part after a long and successful run. During an especially perfunctory performance, Kaufman left the theater and sent him the following telegram: "Watching your performance from the rear of the theater. Wish you were here."

During the run of a play, Kaufman dropped in to monitor a performance. Not at all pleased with what he saw, he placed the following note on the call-board: "Eleven A.M. rehearsal tomorrow morning to remove all improvements to the play inserted since the last rehearsal."

His review of a young tenor, "Guido Nazzo is nazzo guido," began showing up in other notices and was repeated so often that it virtually destroyed the young performer's career. Kaufman was so contrite, he wrote a letter of apology to Mr. Nazzo and offered him a job in a Kaufman musical.

To the author of a badly received play: "I understand your play is full of single entendre."

One of Kaufman's reviews began: "There was laughter in the back of the theater, leading to the belief that someone was telling jokes back there."

In another review he wrote, "I was underwhelmed."

When Kaufman was drama editor at *The New York Times,* a press agent asked, "How do I get our leading lady's name in your newspaper?"

"Shoot her," Kaufman replied.

To the writer of a manuscript replete with spelling errors: "I'm not very good at it myself, but the first rule about spelling is that there is only one *z* in *is.*"

A summer-stock producer who had produced a Kaufman play without paying royalties explained, "After all, it's only a small, insignificant theater."

"Then you'll go to a small, insignificant jail," Kaufman answered.

Moss Hart bought an estate in Bucks County, Pennsylvania, installed a swimming pool and planted hundreds of trees. When Kaufman saw it, he said, "This is what God could have done if He'd had money."

After his great success playing Abraham Lincoln on Broadway, Raymond Massey began to assume the character off the stage, affecting Lincolnesque attire, manner, and speech and prompting Kaufman to observe, "Massey won't be satisfied until someone assassinates him."

Charles Laughton commented that he was successful in the role of Captain Bligh in *Mutiny on the Bounty* because he had come from a seafaring family. "I presume," said Kaufman, alluding to Laughton's portrayal of Quasimodo in *The Hunchback of Notre Dame,* "that you also came from a long line of hunchbacks."

On the television show *This Is Show Business,* a youthful Eddie Fisher complained that girls refused to date him because of his age, and he asked Kaufman's advice. Kaufman replied, "Mr. Fisher, on Mount Wilson there is a telescope that can magnify the most distant stars up to twenty-four times the magnification of any previous telescope. This remarkable instrument was unsurpassed in the world of astronomy until the construction of the Mount Palomar telescope, an even more remarkable instrument of magnification. Owing to advances and improvements in optical technology, it is capable of magnifying the stars to four times the magnification and resolution of the Mount Wilson telescope.

"Mr. Fisher, if you could somehow put the Mount Wilson telescope *inside* the Mount Palomar telescope, you *still* wouldn't be able to detect my interest in your problem."

Kaufman was fired from *This Is Show Business* on December 21, 1952, when he said on the air, "Let's make this one program where no one sings 'Silent Night.'"

QUOTES ON "G"

GAMBLING

Gambling promises the poor what property performs for the rich: that is why the bishops dare not denounce it fundamentally.

GEORGE BERNARD SHAW

GANDHI

It is alarming and also nauseating to see Mr. Gandhi, a seditious Middle Temple lawyer, now posing as a fakir of a type well known in the East, striding half-naked up the steps of the viceregal palace . . . to parley on equal terms with the representatives of the king-emperor.

WINSTON CHURCHILL

GAY

"Gay" used to be one of the most agreeable words in the language. Its appropriation by a notably morose group is an act of piracy.

ARTHUR M. SCHLESINGER, JR.

GENIUS

When a true genius appears in the world you may know him by this sign: that all the dunces are in confederacy against him. JONATHAN SWIFT

GENTILITY

Gentility is what is left over from rich ancestors after the money is gone. JOHN CIARDI

GENTLEMAN

I am a gentleman: I live by robbing the poor.
GEORGE BERNARD SHAW

GERMANY AND THE GERMANS

Germany, the diseased world's bathhouse.
MARK TWAIN

Everything that is ponderous, vicious and pompously clumsy, all long-winded and wearying kinds of style, are developed in great variety among Germans. FRIEDRICH WILHELM NIETZSCHE

German: a good fellow maybe; but it is better to hang him. RUSSIAN PROVERB

GLAMOROUS

Any girl can be glamorous. All you have to do is stand still and look stupid. HEDY LAMARR

GOD

God is the immemorial refuge of the incompetent, the helpless, the miserable. They find not only sanctuary in His arms, but also a kind of superiority, soothing to their macerated egos; He will set them above their betters. H. L. MENCKEN

If God did not exist, it would have been necessary to invent Him. VOLTAIRE

If God created us in his own image we have more than reciprocated. VOLTAIRE

If God were suddenly condemned to live the life
which he has inflicted upon men, He would kill
himself.   ALEXANDRE DUMAS *fils*

> The only excuse for God is that he doesn't exist.
>   STENDHAL

There are scores of thousands of human insects
who are ready at a moment's notice to reveal the
Will of God on every possible subject.
                          GEORGE BERNARD SHAW

> Beware of the man whose God is in the skies.
>   GEORGE BERNARD SHAW

God seems to have left the receiver off the hook
and time is running out.   ARTHUR KOESTLER

> Which is it: is man one of God's blunders, or is
> God one of man's blunders?
>   FRIEDRICH WILHELM NIETZSCHE

God, that dumping ground of our dreams.
                              JEAN ROSTAND

> If you talk to God, you are praying; if God talks
> to you, you have schizophrenia.   THOMAS SZASZ

I cannot believe in a God who wants to be praised
all the time.   FRIEDRICH WILHELM NIETZSCHE

> For me, the single word "God" suggests every-
> thing that is slippery, shady, squalid, foul and
> grotesque.   ANDRÉ BRETON

It takes a long while for a naturally trustful person
to reconcile himself to the idea that after all God
will not help him.   H. L. MENCKEN

God is the Celebrity-Author of the World's Best-
Seller. We have made God into the biggest celebrity of all, to contain our own emptiness.
                                      DANIEL BOORSTIN

God is love, but get it in writing.
                                      GYPSY ROSE LEE

Creator: a comedian whose audience is afraid to
laugh.   H. L. MENCKEN

Imagine the Creator as a low comedian, and at
once the world becomes explicable.
                                      H. L. MENCKEN

I do not believe in God. I believe in cashmere.
                                      FRAN LEBOWITZ

The impotence of God is infinite.
                                      ANATOLE FRANCE

Perhaps God is not dead; perhaps God is himself
mad.   R. D. LAING

God will forgive me; that's his business.
                                      HEINRICH HEINE

He seems to have an inordinate fondness for beetles.
                                      J. B. S. HALDANE

Whom the mad would destroy, first they make
Gods.   BERNARD LEVIN

All Gods *were* immortal.   STANISLAW J. LEC

The worshiper is the father of the gods.
                                    H. L. MENCKEN

_____ GOLDEN RULE _____

The golden rule is that there are no golden rules.
                                    GEORGE BERNARD SHAW

_____ GOLF _____

Golf is a good walk spoiled.   MARK TWAIN

Golf may be played on Sunday, not being a game
within the view of the law, but being a form of
moral effort.   STEPHEN LEACOCK

If I had my way, any man guilty of golf would be
ineligible for any office of trust in the United
States.   H. L. MENCKEN

A game in which you claim the privileges of age,
and retain the playthings of childhood.
                                    SAMUEL JOHNSON

I regard golf as an expensive way of playing marbles.
                                    G. K. CHESTERTON

_____ GOOD _____

To be good, according to the vulgar standard of

goodness, is obviously quite easy. It merely requires a certain amount of sordid terror, a certain lack of imaginative thought, and a certain low passion for middle-class respectability.

OSCAR WILDE

The good die young—because they see it's no use living if you've got to be good.

JOHN BARRYMORE

On the whole human beings want to be good, but not too good and not quite all the time.

GEORGE ORWELL

GOOD BREEDING

Good breeding consists in concealing how much we think of ourselves and how little we think of the other person. MARK TWAIN

GOOD DEED

No good deed goes unpunished.

CLARE BOOTHE LUCE

GOOD AND EVIL

It is almost impossible systematically to constitute a natural moral law. Nature has no principles. She furnishes us with no reason to believe that human life is to be respected. Nature, in her indifference, makes no distinction between good and evil.

ANATOLE FRANCE

GOOD EXAMPLE

Few things are harder to put up with than the
annoyance of a good example.   MARK TWAIN

GOOD LOOKS

She got her good looks from her father. He's a
plastic surgeon.   GROUCHO MARX

GOSSIP

The only thing worse than being talked about is
not being talked about.   OSCAR WILDE

If you can't say anything good about someone, sit
right here by me.

ALICE ROOSEVELT LONGWORTH

GOVERNMENT

A government is the only known vessel that leaks
from the top.   JAMES RESTON

Society is produced by our wants and government
by our wickedness.   THOMAS PAINE

Every government is run by liars and nothing they
say should be believed.   I. F. STONE

In general, the art of government consists in taking as much money as possible from one class of
the citizens to give to the other.   VOLTAIRE

Government is an association of men who do
violence to the rest of us.   LEO TOLSTOY

GRAFFITI

Any academic or literary hustler caught writing that graffiti is a fascinating expression of artistic and cultural creativity [should] be sprayed magenta and left without grants for a year, sentences to be served consecutively.   CALVIN TRILLIN

GRATITUDE

I feel a very unusual sensation—if it is not indigestion, I think it must be gratitude.   BENJAMIN DISRAELI

Gratitude is merely the secret hope of further favors.
FRANÇOIS DE LA ROCHEFOUCAULD

GRIEF

Grief is a species of idleness.   SAMUEL JOHNSON

QUENTIN CRISP

Courtly Curmudgeon

QUENTIN CRISP was born on Christmas Day in 1908 in Sutton, a middle-class suburb of London. He became aware of his homo-sexuality at an early age, and in spite of intense family and social pressure, he has obstinately refused to disguise the fact ever since.

At the age of fourteen he was sent to a typically Spartan English boarding school (which he describes as a combination monastery and prison) where he first encountered the kind of persecution that would plague him all his life.

He worked as a commercial designer and a teacher of tap dancing, wrote books on a variety of subjects including lettering, window dressing, and the English Ministry of Labor, but eventually settled into a thirty-five-year career as an artist's model.

His autobiography, *The Naked Civil Servant,* was published in 1968 and was made into a British television play starring John Hurt. Its success vaulted Mr. Crisp into international celebrity. He has since published five more books: *How to Become a Virgin, How to Have a Lifestyle, Chog, Doing It With Style* (with Donald Carroll), and *Manners From Heaven.*

He became a permanent resident alien in the United States in 1981. He lists his occupation on his income tax forms as "retired waif."

JW: *Your manner is deferential, yet the things you write in your books and essays are scathing indictments of humanity.*
QC: That's what frightens me. Audiences have been known to say that I'm cynical. Now, as you know from reading the work of Mr. Wilde, a cynic is one who knows the price of everything and the value of nothing, and I certainly have been *taught* the price of everything, but I wouldn't say that I didn't appreciate the value of things. What I think worries people is that I can't see any point in an endeavor, a ferocious, prolonged endeavor, to set a permanent "relationship" with anybody. That's the bit I can't understand; there I don't see the value and I do see the price.

JW: *What is the price of a relationship?*

QC: The price is this endless restraint which is asked of you, and the reward is nothing. What have you got in the end of it, unless you have determined to live with somebody rich or more influential than yourself? In fact, that could be a universal law: "The union of two hearts whose incomes are equal is a waste of time."

JW: *Where does love come in?*

QC: There again, we must first agree what "love" is. Are we of one mind that love is the extra effort we make in our dealings with those whom we cannot like? Because that seems to me the very essence of it. I worry when audiences think this is a joke. It's an aphorism, but it isn't a joke. After all, people like yourself belong to the generation which wanted to redistribute the wealth of the world, and half the world's wealth is love. If our love is given to the brave and the beautiful, they will become the millionaires of love. Then what will happen to love's paupers?

JW: *How do you feel about children?*

QC: I treat children exactly as though they're people, and I totally refuse to put on that weird voice that people put on: "How are you, Mr. Smith, and how are you, Mrs. Smith, *and how are you?*" If they think children don't know that they're receiving this nauseous treatment, they're wrong. Very few children want the affection of adults. My parents, at least my mother, imagined that what I wanted was love while I really wanted abject obedience.

JW: *I believe you've written that while your brothers wanted to be footballers, you wanted to be a chronic invalid.*

QC: That's right. I was the youngest, and I knew that my life was, in a sense, a losing battle, and I was right. So I thought there might be some way of making a go of failure. If at first you don't succeed, failure may be your style.

JW: *How did you endure one bashing after another for all those years?*

QC: I was stuck with it. I don't think I could ever have passed myself off as a human being. Long before I ever had the opportunity to dye my hair or pluck my eyebrows—when I was a schoolboy—I was already a lost soul. In England I never left the house without bracing myself. When you're standing at the bus stop and you see half a dozen young men coming along, you know there will be trouble. It's the way the English are.

JW: *You mentioned before that you're working on an article about how to "cure" Christmas.*

QC: Even when I was a child, I was embarrassed by Christmas. First of all, it's my birthday. My mother gave me two shillings to buy a present for my father, and my father gave me two shillings to buy a present for my mother, and they both thanked me! I felt a terrible fool. You get presents you're never going to be able to use, and you have to thank people for them, and they thank *you* for presents *they're* never going to be able to use. Later in life, when I had invented happiness, I ceased to need festivity. In fact, that's a universal law: "Happy people do not need festivity."

JW: *But what's the "cure"?*

QC: The cure, of course, is to simply ignore it. You have to put up with about four years of disgrace when you receive Christmas cards and do not send them, but after that you know that the people who send you Christmas cards are doing it to please *you* and that they don't expect a reply.

JW: *Does your attitude about Christmas extend to religion in general; do you subscribe to the idea that more evil has been done in the name of religion than good?*

QC: Well, it *has* done terrifying things. Religious ideas are inflammatory in a way that I find difficult to understand. There are very few wars over the theory of relativity. Very few heated arguments, for that matter. Whereas, in Northern Ireland, they are killing one another over religion. When I told the people of Northern Ireland that I was an atheist, a woman in the audience stood up and said, "Yes, but is it the God of the Catholics or the God of the Protestants in whom you don't believe?"

JW: *Do you watch television?*

QC: Very little. The programs constantly repeat themselves and one another. No one has yet had the nerve to say, "As we have nothing sensible to tell you between now and eight-thirty, please tune in again then."

JW: *Do you like punk rock?*

QC: I hate it. Long ago I said that all the harm that had come to the world was due to the music, and now someone has arisen and said there will be no more concerts in Central Park because everybody behaved so badly. It seems to me self-evident: All you have to do to restore order to the world is to stop the music. It will mean people will start to speak. One of the girls who rings me up actually said, "If I go to a gathering of strangers and there's no music, I'm embarrassed." That means she would have to speak, or at least listen. They like it loud and they like it dark; they don't want to see and they don't want to hear.

JW: *Why, do you suppose? Does it have anything to do with the Bomb?*

QC: I don't think so, but the Bomb *is* our only friend. I can't see how anyone can think anything else. We've written the equations on the blackboard, and now we've got down to the bottom right-hand corner and it's wrong. The hermit crab has been on the earth for three million years asking nothing, as far as I know, except a few more hermit crabs. Give the world to them. It's only people who've reduced the situation to this.

JW: *Then you think it will end in nuclear destruction?*

QC: Yes, and I think it's right. Never in the history of the world has there been a pileup of arms which have not ultimately been used.

JW: *Isn't it an unprecedented situation? Individuals have always had to confront their own mortality, but they always had the guarantee of posterity—they could leave their works, their children—but now that's been withdrawn. Couldn't that account for the insanity of the second half of the twentieth century? Couldn't that account for punk rock?*

QC: It could, except that the craziness is in the hands of the young, and the young do not think they will die. I can remember, during the war, saying to a woman who ultimately became a nun, "I can't even now get used to the fact that I will die," and she said, "Neither can I, but I practice like mad."

JW: *Do you believe in an afterlife?*

QC: Like most people, I believe not that of which I can be

convinced by logic, I believe what my nature inclines me to believe, and the one thing I wouldn't wish on my worst enemy is eternal life. It also makes old age more acceptable: as it's toward the end of the run, you can overact appallingly.

JW: *Do you like living in New York?*

QC: Yes, I like the people, and I like urban life, even though people are constantly trying to sell me on the countryside. If you want to get out of town occasionally, if fresh air is your lust, fine, but I don't want to spend an *hour* in the country. I don't long for the countryside, *ever*. As a child, I didn't even want to go out-of-doors, let alone go to the country. The outside world was alien to me; I wanted to stay home, even a home so wretched.

JW: *I take it you're happy to be living in the United States. What's your assessment of the American character?*

QC: Americans want to be loved; the English want to be obeyed. In 1963, nothing could have prevented America from ruling the world except what Tennyson called "craven fears of being great." If this building catches on fire and I am the only person who's ever done any fire drill, I must tell you what to do and somebody will die, but if I *don't* tell you what to do, *everybody* will die. This is the position in which America now is. As far as I'm concerned, Korea was an undecided war, and Cuba was an undecided war, and then Vietnam. When Vietnam was first mentioned, I said, "Go out there, measure the place up, send back for a bomb the right size, drop it, and say, 'Oh, it slipped.' Just as well, they're only foreigners."

QUOTES ON "H"

_____ HABIT _____

The fixity of a habit is generally in direct proportion to its absurdity.   MARCEL PROUST

_____ HAPPINESS _____

Happiness, *n*. An agreeable sensation arising from contemplating the misery of another.
                                        AMBROSE BIERCE

Happiness is not something you experience, it's something you remember.   OSCAR LEVANT

Happiness is an imaginary condition, formerly attributed by the living to the dead, now usually attributed by adults to children, and by children to adults.   THOMAS SZASZ

The only really happy folk are married women and single men.   H. L. MENCKEN

Every man is thoroughly happy twice in his life: just after he has met his first love, and just after he has left his last one.   H. L. MENCKEN

Few people can be happy unless they hate some other person, nation, or creed.
                                    BERTRAND RUSSELL

Men can only be happy when they do not assume that the object of life is happiness.
                                        GEORGE ORWELL

Happiness is the perpetual possession of being well deceived.   JONATHAN SWIFT

> I can sympathize with people's pains, but *not* with their pleasure. There is something curiously boring about somebody else's happiness.
>
> ALDOUS HUXLEY

It isn't necessary to be rich and famous to be happy. It's only necessary to be rich.   ALAN ALDA

HATRED

> The more one is hated, I find, the happier one is.
> LOUIS-FERDINAND CÉLINE

Now hatred is by far the longest pleasure;
Men love in haste, but they detest at leisure.
LORD BYRON

> It does not matter much what a man hates provided he hates something.   SAMUEL BUTLER

HEADGEAR

Nobody ought to wear a Greek fisherman's cap who doesn't meet two qualifications:
   1. He is Greek.
   2. He is a fisherman.   ROY BLOUNT, JR.

HEALTH

> The only way to keep your health is to eat what you don't want, drink what you don't like, and do what you'd rather not.   MARK TWAIN

Early to rise and early to bed
Makes a male healthy, wealthy and dead.
JAMES THURBER

HEALTH FOOD

Health food makes me sick.   CALVIN TRILLIN

HEART

My heart is pure as the driven slush.
TALLULAH BANKHEAD

HEAVEN

Heaven, as conventionally conceived, is a place so inane, so dull, so useless, so miserable, that nobody has ever ventured to describe a whole day in heaven, though plenty of people have described a day at the seaside.   GEORGE BERNARD SHAW

If I have any beliefs about immortality, it is that certain dogs I have known will go to heaven, and very, very few persons.   JAMES THURBER

In heaven all the interesting people are missing.
FRIEDRICH WILHELM NIETZSCHE

HEAVEN AND HELL

Men have feverishly conceived a heaven only to find it insipid, and a hell to find it ridiculous.
GEORGE SANTAYANA

HELL

Hell is other people.   JEAN-PAUL SARTRE

When I think of the number of disagreeable people that I know who have gone to a better world, I am sure hell won't be so bad at all.

MARK TWAIN

HEPBURN, AUDREY

A walking X-ray. OSCAR LEVANT

HINDSIGHT

Hindsight is always 20/20. BILLY WILDER

HISTORY

History, *n*. An account mostly false, of events unimportant, which are brought about by rulers mostly knaves, and soldiers mostly fools.

AMBROSE BIERCE

History is a set of lies agreed upon.

NAPOLEON BONAPARTE

History repeats itself; that's one of the things that's wrong with history. CLARENCE DARROW

We learn from history that we do not learn from history. GEORG FRIEDRICH WILHELM HEGEL

History is nothing but a collection of fables and useless trifles, cluttered up with a mass of unnecessary figures and proper names. LEO TOLSTOY

On the whole history tends to be rather poor fiction—except at its best. GORE VIDAL

History is a bucket of ashes.   CARL SANDBURG

History is nothing but a pack of tricks that we play upon the dead.   VOLTAIRE

History is a nightmare from which we are trying to awaken.   JAMES JOYCE

History would be a wonderful thing—if it were only true.   LEO TOLSTOY

History is bunk.   HENRY FORD

HISTORIAN

Historian: an unsuccessful novelist.

H. L. MENCKEN

HOLIDAY

Holidays are an expensive trial of strength. The only satisfaction comes from survival.

JONATHAN MILLER

HOLISTIC

I've decided to skip "holistic." I don't know what it means, and I don't want to know. That may seem extreme, but I followed the same strategy toward "Gestalt" and the Twist, and lived to tell the tale.   CALVIN TRILLIN

HOLLYWOOD

Hollywood is a place where people from Iowa mistake each other for movie stars.

FRED ALLEN

Strip away the phony tinsel of Hollywood and you find the real tinsel underneath.

OSCAR LEVANT

I've been asked if I ever get the DTs; I don't know; it's hard to tell where Hollywood ends and the DTs begin. W. C. FIELDS

Hollywood is a sewer with service from the Ritz Carlton. WILSON MIZNER

The only "ism" Hollywood believes in is plagiarism.

DOROTHY PARKER

Over in Hollywood they almost made a great picture, but they caught it in time.

WILSON MIZNER

In Hollywood, if you don't have happiness, you send out for it. REX REED

Good evening, ladies and gentlemen—and welcome to darkest Hollywood. Night brings a stillness to the jungle. It is so quiet you can hear a name drop. The savage beasts have already begun gathering at the water holes to quench their thirst. Now one should be especially alert. The vicious table-hopper is on the prowl and the spotted backbiter may lurk behind a potted palm.

ALFRED HITCHCOCK

You can take all the sincerity in Hollywood, place it in the navel of a fruit fly and still have room enough for three caraway seeds and a producer's heart. FRED ALLEN

Hollywood is a great place if you're an orange.
FRED ALLEN

Hollywood is like being nowhere and talking to nobody about nothing.
MICHELANGELO ANTONIONI

A dreary industrial town controlled by hoodlums of enormous wealth.
S. J. PERELMAN

HOLY ROMAN EMPIRE

The Holy Roman Empire was neither holy, nor Roman, nor an Empire.
VOLTAIRE

HONESTY

It's better to be quotable than to be honest.
TOM STOPPARD

HOPE

Hope in reality is the worst of all evils, because it prolongs the torments of man.
FRIEDRICH WILHELM NIETZSCHE

HOSPITALITY

People are far more sincere and good-humored at speeding their parting guests than on meeting them.
ANTON CHEKHOV

HUMAN

There are times when you have to choose between being human and having good taste.
BERTOLT BRECHT

Humanity is a pigsty where liars, hypocrites and
the obscene in spirit congregate.

GEORGE MOORE

_____ HUMAN CONDITION _____

He who despairs over an event is a coward, but he
who holds hopes for the human condition is a
fool.   ALBERT CAMUS

We all live in a house on fire, no fire department
to call; no way out, just the upstairs window to
look out of while the fire burns the house down
with us trapped, locked in it.

TENNESSEE WILLIAMS

He who has never envied the vegetable has missed
the human drama.   E. M. CIORAN

The basic fact about human existence is not that it
is a tragedy, but that it is a bore.

H. L. MENCKEN

_____ HUMAN NATURE _____

The nature of men and women—their *essential
nature*—is so vile and despicable that if you were
to portray a person as he really is, no one would
believe you.   W. SOMERSET MAUGHAM

A man never reaches that dizzy height of wisdom
that he can no longer be led by the nose.

MARK TWAIN

It is easier to denature plutonium than to denature
the evil spirit of man. ALBERT EINSTEIN

It is human nature to think wisely and act foolishly.
ANATOLE FRANCE

No doubt Jack the Ripper excused himself on the
grounds that it was human nature. A. A. MILNE

―――――――――――――― HUMAN RACE ――――――――――――――

If I could get my membership fee back, I'd resign
from the human race. FRED ALLEN

Don't overestimate the decency of the human race.
H. L. MENCKEN

Their heart's in the right place, but their head is a
thoroughly inefficient organ.
W. SOMERSET MAUGHAM

The chief obstacle to the progress of the human
race is the human race. DON MARQUIS

―――――――――――――― HUMILITY ――――――――――――――

Humility is no substitute for a good personality.
FRAN LEBOWITZ

―――――――――――――― HUMOR ――――――――――――――

Humor is emotional chaos remembered in tran-
quility. JAMES THURBER

When a man wants to murder a tiger he calls it
sport; when a tiger wants to murder him he calls it
ferocity.   GEORGE BERNARD SHAW

> A sportsman is a man who, every now and then,
> simply has to out and kill something.
> STEPHEN LEACOCK

The English country gentleman galloping after a
fox—the unspeakable in full pursuit of the uneatable.
OSCAR WILDE

> The fascination of shooting as a sport depends
> almost wholly on whether you are at the right or
> wrong end of the gun.   P. G. WODEHOUSE

The husband who wants a happy marriage should
learn to keep his mouth shut and his checkbook
open.   GROUCHO MARX

> Husbands never become good; they merely be-
> come proficient.   H. L. MENCKEN

The majority of husbands remind me of an orang-
utan trying to play the violin.
HONORÉ DE BALZAC

> A woman usually respects her father, but her view
> of her husband is mingled with contempt, for she
> is of course privy to the transparent devices by
> which she snared him.   H. L. MENCKEN

A husband is what's left of the lover once the
nerve has been extracted.

HELEN ROWLAND

A woman who takes her husband about with her
everywhere is like a cat that goes on playing with a
mouse long after she's killed it.   SAKI

LADY ASTOR: If you were my husband, Winston,
I'd put poison in your tea.
WINSTON CHURCHILL: If I were your husband,
Nancy, I'd drink it.

_____ HYPOCRISY _____

An ounce of hypocrisy is worth a pound of
ambition.   MICHAEL KORDA

KARL KRAUS

Word and Substance and Empty Chairs

KARL KRAUS, the Viennese dramatist, critic, and satirist, was born in 1874 in a small Bohemian town near Prague to well-to-do Jewish parents. Three years later the family moved to Vienna, where Kraus spent the rest of his life.

He became a writer when a spinal deformity prevented him from realizing his childhood ambition of entering the theater. He contributed acerbic critical essays to Viennese publications and turned down an offer to join the prestigious Viennese daily, *Neue Freie Presse,* to avoid becoming what he termed a "culture clown."

He continued to publish polemics against the intellectuals, literati, financiers, politicians, poets, and journalists he deemed responsible for the moral bankruptcy of Europe. His avowed object was no less than the preservation of civilization, which he saw imperiled by the cozy relationship between the Austrian press and intellectuals. He was a consummate rhetorician who equated morality with purity of language. ("Word and substance—that is the only connection I have striven for in my life.") He assailed the deliberate corruption of language by special interests and railed against what might be termed the artistic-journalistic complex of the time.

He was acquainted with Sigmund Freud and expressed a fondness for him personally but became obsessed with what he considered the chicanery of psychoanalysis. He attacked Freud and his disciples, whom he dubbed "soul doctors" and "psychoanals." He wrote of Freud's critique of Michelangelo: "Analysis is the *schnorrer's* [beggar's] need to explain how riches come to be; whatever he doesn't possess must have been acquired by swindle; the other merely has the fortune; he, fortunately, *knows.*"

In 1899, he founded his own magazine, *Die Fackel (The Torch),* with which he relentlessly assaulted the corruption and hypocrisy of European society. In it he denounced prison conditions, price fixing, child labor abuses, and the unequal treatment of women. Initially there were other contributors, including August Strindberg and Heinrich Mann, but from 1911 until his death in 1936, Kraus was its sole contributor. ("I no longer have collaborators. I used to be envious of them. They repel those readers whom I want to lose myself.")

Die Fackel contained no paid advertisements and professed indifference to its readers; this announcement appeared regularly on its back cover:

> It is requested that no books, periodicals, invitations, clippings, leaflets, manuscripts or written information of any sort be sent in. No such material will ever be returned, nor will any letters be answered. Any return postage that may be enclosed will be turned over to charity.

Kraus wrote poetry in which he attempted to objectify his stringent concept of language, and several plays, including *Die letzen Tage der Menschheit (The Last Days of Mankind)* in 1922, which portrayed the disintegration of European society and prophesied the Second World War. From 1910 until his death, he gave numerous public readings of his own works to enthusiastic audiences all over Europe.

His attitude isolated him from all but a few close friends. He slept days and worked nights and abhorred invasions of his privacy. He recoiled when people accosted him on the street and went to great lengths to avoid human contact. He died of heart failure in June 1936, less than two years before the German *Anschluss,* an event that confirmed his dire predictions for the future of Austrian society. The irony of his work as a satirist was that his contemporaries were so ridiculously self-satisfied, they didn't know they were being savaged.

Kraus was an early champion of the poet and playwright Bertolt Brecht, who said of him: "When the age died by its own hand, he was that hand." Erich Heller appraised him thus: "The satiric radicalism of Karl Kraus is only a defense mechanism of a man ardently in love with the beauty and joy of living."

KARL KRAUS ON THE
LIFE OF A MISANTHROPE

I and my public understand each other very well:
it does not hear what I say, and I don't say what it
wants to hear.

———————

If I return people's greetings, I do so only to give
them their greeting back.

———————

Many desire to kill me, and many wish to spend
an hour chatting with me. The law protects me
from the former.

———————

What torture, this life in society! Often someone
is obliging enough to offer me a light, and in
order to oblige *him* I have to fish a cigarette out of
my pocket.

———————

One's need for loneliness is not satisfied if one sits
at a table alone. There must be empty chairs as
well. If the waiter takes away a chair on which no
one is sitting, I feel a void and my sociability is
aroused. I can't live without empty chairs.

KARL KRAUS ON LITERATURE

In the beginning was the review copy, and a man received it from the publisher. Then he wrote a review. Then he wrote a book which the publisher accepted and sent on to someone else as a review copy. The man who received it did likewise. This is how modern literature came into being.

Most critics write critiques which are by the authors they write critiques about. That would not be so bad, but then most authors write works which are by the critics who write critiques about them.

To write a novel may be pure pleasure. To live a novel presents certain difficulties. As for reading a novel, I do my best to get out of it.

I have decided many a stylistic problem first by head, then by heads or tails.

Heinrich Heine so loosened the corsets of the German language that today every little salesman can fondle her breasts.

The making of a journalist: no ideas and the ability to express them.

Journalists write because they have nothing to say, and have something to say because they write.

A plagiarist should be made to copy the author a hundred times.

Today's literature: prescriptions written by patients.

KARL KRAUS ON PSYCHOANALYSIS

Psychoanalysis is the mental illness it purports to cure.

────────

So-called psychoanalysis is the occupation of lascivious rationalists who reduce everything in the world to sexual causes, with the exception of their occupation.

────────

Psychoanalysis: a rabbit that was swallowed by a boa constrictor that just wanted to see what it was like in there.

────────

An analyst turns a man to dust.

────────

Psychoanalysts are father confessors who like to listen to the sins of the fathers as well.

────────

One cleans someone else's threshold of consciousness only if one's own home is dirty.

Most people are sick. But only few know that this is something they can be proud of. These are the psychoanalysts.

They have the press, they have the stock exchange, they also have the subconscious!

They pick our dreams as though they were our pockets.

QUOTES ON "I"

IDEAS

To die for an idea is to set a rather high price on
conjecture. ANATOLE FRANCE

To die for an idea; it is unquestionably noble. But
how much nobler it would be if men died for
ideas that were true! H. L. MENCKEN

We use ideas merely to justify our evil, and speech
merely to conceal our ideas. VOLTAIRE

The history of ideas is the history of the grudges
of solitary men. E. M. CIORAN

IDEALISM

Idealism is the noble toga that political gentlemen
drape over their will to power. ALDOUS HUXLEY

Idealism is fine, but as it approaches reality the
cost becomes prohibitive.

WILLIAM F. BUCKLEY, JR.

Idealism increases in direct proportion to one's
distance from the problem. JOHN GALSWORTHY

An idealist is one who, on noticing that a rose
smells better than a cabbage, concludes that it will
also make better soup. H. L. MENCKEN

I'm an idealist: I don't know where I'm going but
I'm on my way. CARL SANDBURG

When they come down from their ivory towers,
idealists are apt to walk straight into the gutter.
LOGAN PEARSALL SMITH

The idealist is incorrigible—if he is turned out of
his heaven, he makes an ideal of his hell.
FRIEDRICH WILHELM NIETZSCHE

The idealist walks on his toes, the materialist on
his talons. MALCOLM DE CHAZAL

————————— IMMACULATE CONCEPTION —————————

I went to a convent in New York and was fired
finally for my insistence that the Immaculate Conception was spontaneous combustion.
DOROTHY PARKER

————————————— IMMORALITY —————————————

Immorality: the morality of those who are having
a better time. H. L. MENCKEN

————————————— IMMORTALITY—————————————

Immortality is the condition of a dead man who
doesn't believe he is dead. H.L. MENCKEN

Millions long for immortality who do not know
what to do with themselves on a rainy Sunday
afternoon. SUSAN ERTZ

I don't want to achieve immortality through my
work. I want to achieve it through not dying.
WOODY ALLEN

Impiety, *n*. Your irreverence toward my deity.
                                        AMBROSE BIERCE

_____ INCOME _____

It is better to have a permanent income than to be
fascinating.   OSCAR WILDE

_____ INFLATION _____

Inflation is the one form of taxation that can be
imposed without legislation.   MILTON FRIEDMAN

A dollar saved is a quarter earned.   JOHN CIARDI

_____ INSANITY _____

Insanity: a perfectly rational adjustment to the
insane world.   R. D. LAING

_____ INSINCERITY _____

What people call insincerity is simply a method by
which we can multiply our personalities.
                                        OSCAR WILDE

_____ INTELLIGENCE _____

I would like to take you seriously but to do so
would affront your intelligence.
                              WILLIAM F. BUCKLEY, JR.

_____ INTERVIEW _____

The interview is an intimate conversation between
journalist and politician wherein the journalist seeks

to take advantage of the garrulity of the politician
and the politician of the credulity of the journalist.
EMERY KELEN

━━━━━━━━━━━━━━ INVITATION ━━━━━━━━━━━━━━

> I must decline your invitation owing to a subse-
> quent engagement.   OSCAR WILDE

━━━━━━━━━━━━ IRELAND AND THE IRISH ━━━━━━━━━━━━

Ireland has the honor of being the only country
which never persecuted the Jews—because she never
let them in.   JAMES JOYCE

> I showed my appreciation of my native land in the
> usual Irish way by getting out of it as soon as I
> possibly could.   GEORGE BERNARD SHAW

The Irish are a fair people—they never speak well
of one another.   SAMUEL JOHNSON

QUOTES ON "J"

If my theory of relativity is proven successful, Germany will claim me as a German and France will declare that I am a citizen of the world. Should my theory prove untrue, France will say that I am a German, and Germany will declare that I am a Jew.   ALBERT EINSTEIN

The Jews are a frightened people. Nineteen centuries of Christian love have broken down their nerves.
ISRAEL ZANGWILL

JOGGING

It's unnatural for people to run around city streets unless they are thieves or victims. It makes people nervous to see someone running. I know that when I see someone running on my street, my instincts tell me to let the dog out after him.
MIKE ROYKO

JOURNALISM

Journalism justifies its own existence by the great Darwinian principle of the survival of the vulgarist.
OSCAR WILDE

There is much to be said in favor of modern journalism. By giving us the opinions of the uneducated, it keeps us in touch with the ignorance of the community.   OSCAR WILDE

Journalism consists largely in saying "Lord Jones died" to people who never knew Lord Jones was alive. G. K. CHESTERTON

Journalism is the ability to meet the challenge of filling space. REBECCA WEST

_____ JUDGMENT _____

We should all be obliged to appear before a board every five years and justify our existence . . . on pain of liquidation. GEORGE BERNARD SHAW

_____ JURY _____

Jury: a group of twelve men who, having lied to the judge about their hearing, health and business engagements, have failed to fool him.
H. L. MENCKEN

A jury consists of twelve persons chosen to decide who has the better lawyer. ROBERT FROST

Wretches hang that jurymen may dine.
ALEXANDER POPE

_____ JUSTICE _____

Justice, *n*. A commodity which in a more or less adulterated condition the State sells to the citizen as a reward for his allegiance, taxes and personal service. AMBROSE BIERCE

Justice is the sanction of established injustice.
ANATOLE FRANCE

In the Halls of Justice the only justice is in the halls. LENNY BRUCE

QUOTES ON "K"

Every country should have at least one King Farouk.
GORE VIDAL

KILLING

Kill one man and you are a murderer. Kill millions and you are a conqueror. Kill all and you are a God.
JEAN ROSTAND

KINDNESS

One can always be kind to people about whom one cares nothing.
OSCAR WILDE

KISS

The kiss originated when the first male reptile licked the first female reptile, implying in a subtle, complimentary way that she was as succulent as the small reptile he had for dinner the night before.
F. SCOTT FITZGERALD

KNOWLEDGE

To know all is not to forgive all. It is to despise everybody.
QUENTIN CRISP

PAUL FUSSELL

He Cries at the Indy 500

PAUL FUSSELL (pronounced *fŭs̆ əl*) was born in Pasadena, California, in 1924. He received a B.A. from Pomona College in 1947, and an M.A. and a Ph.D. from Harvard in 1949 and 1952. He has taught at Connecticut College, the University of Heidelberg, Rutgers University, and the University of Pennsylvania, where he has been the Donald T. Regan Professor of English Literature since 1983.

He is the author of ten books on a wide range of subjects,

including *Abroad: British Literary Traveling Between the Wars; The Great War and Modern Memory,* which received the National Book Award in 1976; and *Class,* an insouciant indictment of the American class system. His literary criticism appears frequently in *Harper's* and *The New Republic,* both of which he serves as a contributing editor.

JW: *Are you a curmudgeon?*
PF: I don't like the word *curmudgeon.* It implies that there's something wrong with social and cultural criticism, which is the obligation of every educated person. If every educated person is to be a curmudgeon, fine. Certain people have to *notice* things.

There's a great essay by George Orwell called "Why I Write," in which he says that every writer who is honest is motivated by two things: one, the desire to show off; and two, the *habit of noticing unpleasant facts.* Anybody who notices unpleasant facts in the have-a-nice-day world we live in is going to be designated a curmudgeon.
JW: *You see the curmudgeon as a reformer?*
PF: Yes, he wants things to be better. Instead of running for Congress he works through public presentation. He annoys and amuses people in order to bring about social change. The so-called curmudgeon is really an idealist, perhaps even a romantic, sentimental idealist.
JW: *I hear a lot about the cynicism and materialism of students these days.*
PF: They're the same as they always were. I've been in this trade

for thirty-five years, and I don't see much difference. Almost none of them are going to the university for the right reasons, but gradually the best of them wake up. Nobody eighteen has any shape yet, men or women. You're trying to help them see, and you don't know whether you've succeeded until they're thirty-five.

JW: *You've said that this is "the worst time since the thirteenth century . . . the terrorism, the brutality, the contempt for human life, a very vicious place to live, this century." What else do you find contemptible about it?*

PF: I think the moment is notable for a general lack of attention to human dignity, which is as bad as it's been since the Renaissance. What I dislike most about the contemporary scene is the way people are treated like animals, which I think we owe to the Second World War—not just the Holocaust but the army too. Living today is like being in the army: You line up for everything, you *queue.*

What I hate about contemporary life is a deep, unimaginative contempt for human beings *disguised as friendly concern.* If it weren't for this fraud, this pretense of friendliness, I could tolerate it easier. I would much rather have people say, "Look, you *shit,* line up there, we don't give a *fuck* about you and your mean bank account." There's no reason to be uncomfortable just because those people want you to be uncomfortable. There's too little opposition to this.

JW: *Why?*

PF: I think most people secretly like being treated badly, perhaps because it makes them feel like part of a great big industrial enterprise, that they're somehow *contributing* to the modern world.

Another thing that disturbs me is what I call "technological pretension." Every day I spend half an hour to an hour clearing up the mistakes of people I have business relations with—the telephone company, the bank, everybody. I moved recently, and half the people who received the change-of-address card got it wrong because they're so technologically pretentious with their little computer keyboards.

JW: *Are you against machines per se?*

PF: No, but I'm getting a little bit off them because I don't think they're opening up the good life at all. They're making slaves of people. I got rid of my car, for example. What I'm against is a certain attitude about people that makes machines inevitable. Machines have no sense of humor, and I can't stand to live in a world with no sense of humor, no sense of irony, where everything is literal. That's hell.

JW: *In that context you've written that by the next century there will be no difference between the United States and the Soviet Union.*

PF: Yes, we're getting closer all the time. I call it "prole drift." It's probably a result of the world population problem—the population of the world has *doubled* since I was a boy. But intelligence hasn't doubled; sensitivity hasn't doubled; everything that matters hasn't doubled. It's an immense overcrowding. Hence lines and identification numbers are on the increase everywhere, and I think that's worth objecting to.

And the two societies are becoming identical in terms of athleticism, the idea of finding national identity in athletic victory.

The Soviets happen to be good at chess and weight lifting and we're good at football, but it's the same kind of stupid, mind-blowing imbecility on both sides which is projected as national policy. Two great big, muscle-bound giants with little pea brains on top.

JW: *What else disturbs you about contemporary American life?*

PF: First-naming by people who have no right to do it. People phone me from Dallas and Houston—they always mispronounce my last name as "few-sell," and that tips me off immediately—and they'll say, "Paul, I'm selling some wonderful oil shares out here and—" Click.

JW: *Is the process of having your work published an adversarial relationship?*

PF: Very much, and I get angry when editors and publishers try to be my friends. It indicates that they're about to swindle you.

JW: *You've written extensively about class. For example, you've said that chess is rarely found above the upper middle class.*

PF: I have never known an upper-class person to play chess. Backgammon's their game. Another thing: We've had a young relative staying with us for the past few days which required me to cede her my bathroom and use another one. I was uncomfortable for the entire time, and it reminded me that the upper class never allows itself to be uncomfortable, except on a yacht.

JW: *You did a piece for* Harper's *about the Indianapolis 500 in which you confessed that you cried when they played "Back Home in Indiana."*

PF: I do it at weddings too. I think it has to do with my long relation with young people as an observer of their hopes and their beliefs. Seeing someone who really believes in something makes me cry, I don't know why. Out of curiosity, I've visited great Catholic religious centers like Fatima in Portugal and Lourdes in France, although I'm a total religious skeptic myself, as a sort of sociologist of that pathology. It always makes me cry to see the pathos of people who actually believe that drinking holy water is going to cure their polio.

JW: *You've done a lot of traveling and travel writing, from which I gather you didn't like Tel Aviv.*

PF: I think Tel Aviv is an awful place. It apes the worst things about the United States. It's full of fast food, piped music, and fraudulent friendliness. Everything I hate about the United States, Tel Aviv has in spades. But it's not just Tel Aviv; I could point to many other places in the world that have done this to themselves.

JW: *In your book,* Abroad, *you say that "Anyone who has hotel reservations and speaks no French is a tourist." How do you feel about the French?*

PF: I adore them because they're very honest in their snot. They don't pretend to like anybody but themselves. I love that. I love the French restaurant and the French shop where everyone is addressed as *Monsieur* or *Madame,* regardless of their social class. They erect an iron curtain of formality between themselves and other people. I find that I'm happier in an environment like that than in a pseudo-friendly one like the United States. I've never had a French taxi driver try to become my friend.

JW: *Whereas here . . .*

PF: Sometimes when I'm in a cruel mood and I'm being driven

back from the airport by a taxi driver and he says, "How about those Eagles?" I'll say something like, "What the fuck is this Eagles stuff?" He assumes that because he has me in his cab I have the same interests as he does. I don't demand that he know all about *Samson Agonistes*, yet he demands that I know all about the Eagles.

JW: *Aside from that, how do you like living in Philadelphia?*

PF: The most accurate thing I can say about Philadelphia, from the point of view of somebody who knows New York and London, is that it's *sweet*. When I want excitement, I go to New York for a heavy day or evening and then I come back to the dormitory. This is quietville.

QUOTES ON "L"

LAUGHTER

Laughter, while it lasts, slackens and unbraces the mind, weakens the faculties, and causes a kind of remissness and dissolution in all the powers of the soul.

JOSEPH ADDISON

Laughter is nothing else but sudden glory arising from some sudden conception of some eminency in ourselves, by comparison with the infirmity of others, or with our own formerly.

THOMAS HOBBES

Perhaps I know best why it is man alone who laughs; he alone suffers so deeply that he had to invent laughter.

FRIEDRICH WILHELM NIETZSCHE

He who laughs has not yet heard the bad news.

BERTOLT BRECHT

LAW

The law, in its majestic equality, forbids the rich as well as the poor to sleep under bridges, to beg in the streets, and to steal bread. ANATOLE FRANCE

The penalty for laughing in a courtroom is six months in jail; if it were not for this penalty, the jury would never hear the evidence.

H. L. MENCKEN

Law is a bottomless pit; it is a cormorant, a harpy that devours everything. JONATHAN SWIFT

I learned law so well, the day I graduated I sued the college, won the case, and got my tuition back.   FRED ALLEN

> Every law is an infraction of liberty.
> JEREMY BENTHAM

—————————— LAWSUIT ——————————

Lawsuit, *n*. A machine which you go into as a pig and come out of as a sausage.   AMBROSE BIERCE

> I was never ruined but twice: once when I lost a lawsuit, and once when I won one.   VOLTAIRE

—————————— LAWYERS ——————————

Lawyer, *n*. One skilled in the circumvention of the law.   AMBROSE BIERCE

> Lawyer: one who protects us against robbery by taking away the temptation.   H. L. MENCKEN

Lawyers are the only persons in whom ignorance of the law is not punished.
JEREMY BENTHAM

> If law school is so hard to get through . . . how come there are so many lawyers? CALVIN TRILLIN

Lawyers, I suppose, were children once.
CHARLES LAMB

> Lawyers are . . . operators of the toll bridge which anyone in search of justice must pass.
> JANE BRYANT QUINN

—————————————— LAZINESS ——————————————

Laziness is nothing more than the habit of resting
before you get tired.   JULES RENARD

—————————————— LEISURE ——————————————

The secret of being miserable is to have the leisure
to bother about whether you are happy or not.
                            GEORGE BERNARD SHAW

—————————————— LIAR ——————————————

The aim of the liar is simply to charm, to delight,
to give pleasure. He is the very basis of civilized
society.   OSCAR WILDE

It is always the best policy to tell the truth, unless,
of course, you are an exceptionally good liar.
                            JEROME K. JEROME

—————————————— LIBERAL ——————————————

A liberal is a man who leaves a room when the
fight begins.   HEYWOOD BROUN

The liberals can understand everything but people
who don't understand them.   LENNY BRUCE

Liberal: a power worshipper without power.
                                GEORGE ORWELL

A liberal is a person whose interests aren't at stake
at the moment.   WILLIS PLAYER

A liberal is a man too broadminded to take his
own side in a quarrel.   ROBERT FROST

Hell hath no fury like a liberal scorned.
DICK GREGORY

────────────────────── LIBERTY ──────────────────────

Liberty means responsibility; that is why most men dread it.   GEORGE BERNARD SHAW

Liberty doesn't work as well in practice as it does in speeches.   WILL ROGERS

Liberty is the right to do whatever the law permits.
CHARLES LOUIS MONTESQUIEU

────────────────────── LIFE ──────────────────────

Life is a disease; and the only difference between one man and another is the stage of the disease at which he lives.   GEORGE BERNARD SHAW

Life is an effort that deserves a better cause.
KARL KRAUS

Life does not cease to be funny when people die any more than it ceases to be serious when people laugh.   GEORGE BERNARD SHAW

Life is a hospital in which every patient is possessed by the desire of changing his bed. One would prefer to suffer near the fire, and another is certain he would get well if he were by the window.
CHARLES BAUDELAIRE

Life is not so bad if you have plenty of luck, a good physique and not too much imagination.
CHRISTOPHER ISHERWOOD

Life is one long process of getting tired.
SAMUEL BUTLER

Life is not a spectacle or a feast; it is a predicament.
GEORGE SANTAYANA

Why shouldn't things be largely absurd, futile, and transitory? They are so, and we are so, and they and we go very well together.
GEORGE SANTAYANA

Life is a predicament which precedes death.
HENRY JAMES

Life is a zoo in a jungle.   PETER DE VRIES

Human life is a flash of occasional enjoyments lighting up a mass of pain and misery, a bagatelle of transient experience.
ALFRED NORTH WHITEHEAD

We are all serving a life sentence in the dungeon of life.   CYRIL CONNOLLY

Life is a constant oscillation between the sharp horns of a dilemma.   H. L. MENCKEN

Life is a crowded superhighway with bewildering cloverleaf exits on which a man is liable to find himself speeding back in the direction he came.
PETER DE VRIES

Life is a dead-end street.   H. L. MENCKEN

People say that life is the thing, but I prefer reading.
LOGAN PEARSALL SMITH

Life is gamble at terrible odds; if it was a bet you wouldn't take it.   TOM STOPPARD

Life is like an onion: you peel off layer after layer and then you find there is nothing in it.
JAMES GIBBONS HUNEKER

In the great game of human life one begins by being a dupe and ends by being a rogue.
VOLTAIRE

Life is divided into the horrible and the miserable.
WOODY ALLEN

The first half of our life is ruined by our parents and the second half by our children.
CLARENCE DARROW

Life is far too important a thing ever to talk seriously about.   OSCAR WILDE

The meaning of life is that it stops.
FRANZ KAFKA

Life is judged with all the blindness of life itself.
GEORGE SANTAYANA

Life can little else supply
But a few good fucks and then we die.
JOHN WILKES

Life is an unbroken succession of false situations.
THORNTON WILDER

Life is something to do when you can't get to
sleep.   FRAN LEBOWITZ

Life is nothing but a competition to be the criminal rather than the victim.   BERTRAND RUSSELL

Life is a God-damned, stinking, treacherous game
and nine hundred and ninety-nine men out of a
thousand are bastards.   THEODORE DREISER

──────────── LITERARY PARTY ────────────

A traffic jam of the lost waiting for the ferry
across the Styx.   DELMORE SCHWARTZ

──────────── LITERATURE ────────────

Literature: proclaiming in front of everyone what
one is careful to conceal from one's immediate
circle.   JEAN ROSTAND

──────────── LITIGATION ────────────

For certain people, after fifty, litigation takes the
place of sex.   GORE VIDAL

──────────── LOATHINGS ────────────

My loathings are simple: stupidity, oppression,
crime, cruelty, soft music.   VLADIMIR NABOKOV

──────────── LONDON ────────────

London, that great cesspool into which all the
loungers of the Empire are irresistibly drained.
                            ARTHUR CONAN DOYLE

A place you go to get bronchitis.
FRAN LEBOWITZ

London, like a bowl of viscid human fluid, boils sullenly over the rim of its encircling hills and slops messily and uglily into the home counties.
H. G. WELLS

A foggy, dead-alive city like a dying ant-heap. London was created for rich young men to shop in, dine in, ride in, get married in, go to theatres in, and die in as respected householders. It is a city for the unmarried upper class, not for the poor.
CYRIL CONNOLLY

Crowds without company, and dissipation without pleasure. EDWARD GIBBON

The monstrous tuberosity of civilized life, the capital of England. THOMAS CARLYLE

LOS ANGELES

Thought is barred in this city of Dreadful Joy, and conversation is unknown. ALDOUS HUXLEY

I mean, who would want to live in a place where the only cultural advantage is that you can turn right on a red light. WOODY ALLEN

Isn't it nice that people who prefer Los Angeles to San Francisco live there? HERB CAEN

A big hard-boiled city with no more personality than a paper cup. RAYMOND CHANDLER

There is always something so delightfully real about what is phony here. And something so phony about what is real. A sort of disreputable senility.

NOEL COWARD

Everything in Los Angeles is too large, too loud and usually banal in concept . . . The plastic asshole of the world.

WILLIAM FAULKNER

The town is like an advertisement for itself; none of its charms are left to the visitor's imagination.

CHRISTOPHER ISHERWOOD

L.A.: where there's never weather, and walking is a crime. L.A.: where the streetlights and palm trees go on forever, where darkness never comes, like a deal that never goes down, a meeting that's never taken. The city of angels: where every cockroach has a screenplay and even the winos wear roller skates. It's that kind of town.

IAN SHOALES

LOTTERY

I figure you have the same chance of winning the lottery whether you play or not.

FRAN LEBOWITZ

LOVE

Love is the delightful interval between meeting a beautiful girl and discovering that she looks like a haddock.

JOHN BARRYMORE

Love is the most subtle form of self-interest.

HOLBROOK JACKSON

Love is something that hangs up behind the bathroom door and smells of Lysol.

ERNEST HEMINGWAY

Love is the state in which man sees things most decidedly as they are not.

FRIEDRICH WILHELM NIETZSCHE

A temporary insanity curable by marriage.

AMBROSE BIERCE

The delusion that one woman differs from another.

H. L. MENCKEN

People who are not in love fail to understand how an intelligent man can suffer because of a very ordinary woman. This is like being surprised that anyone should be stricken with cholera because of a creature so insignificant as the common bacillus.

MARCEL PROUST

First love is a kind of vaccination which saves a man from catching the complaint a second time.

HONORÉ DE BALZAC

In the Forties, to get a girl you had to be a GI or a jock. In the Fifties, to get a girl you had to be Jewish. In the Sixties, to get a girl you had to be black. In the Seventies, to get a girl you've got to be a girl.

MORT SAHL

Love is so much better when you are not married.

MARIA CALLAS

Many a man in love with a dimple makes the
mistake of marrying the whole girl.
STEPHEN LEACOCK

> By the time you swear you're his,
> Shivering and sighing,
> And he vows his passion is
> Infinite, undying—
> One of you is lying.
>
> DOROTHY PARKER

Many a man has fallen in love with a girl in a light
so dim he would not have chosen a suit by it.
MAURICE CHEVALIER

> LOVE: A word properly applied to our delight in
> particular kinds of food; sometimes metaphori-
> cally spoken of the favorite objects of all our
> appetites.   HENRY FIELDING

Once love is purged of vanity, it resembles a feeble
convalescent, hardly able to drag itself about.
NICOLAS CHAMFORT

> It is a mistake to speak of a bad choice in love,
> since as soon as a choice exists, it can only be bad.
> MARCEL PROUST

The duration of passion is proportionate with the
original resistance of the woman.
HONORÉ DE BALZAC

> It's possible to love a human being if you don't
> know them too well.   CHARLES BUKOWSKI

The Art of Love: knowing how to combine the temperament of a vampire with the discretion of an anemone.   E. M. CIORAN

Love, love, love—all the wretched cant of it, masking egotism, lust, masochism, fantasy under a mythology of sentimental postures, a welter of self-induced miseries and joys, blinding and masking the essential personalities in the frozen gestures of courtship, in the kissing and the dating and the desire, the compliments and the quarrels which vivify its barrenness.   GERMAINE GREER

Love is only a dirty trick played on us to achieve the continuation of the species.
        W. SOMERSET MAUGHAM

To be in love is merely to be in a state of perceptual anesthesia.   H. L. MENCKEN

Love is the desire to prostitute oneself.
        CHARLES BAUDELAIRE

The credulity of love is the most fundamental source of authority.   SIGMUND FREUD

Love is a gross exaggeration of the difference between one person and everybody else.
        GEORGE BERNARD SHAW

Love is the victim's response to the rapist.
        TI-GRACE ATKINSON

Love, in present day society, is just the exchange of two momentary desires and the contact of two skins.   NICOLAS CHAMFORT

Love: a burnt match skating in a urinal.
                                        HART CRANE

Love is what happens to a man and a woman who don't know each other.
                        W. SOMERSET MAUGHAM

I can understand companionship. I can understand bought sex in the afternoon. I cannot understand the love affair.   GORE VIDAL

Love as a relation between men and women was ruined by the desire to make sure of the legitimacy of children.   BERTRAND RUSSELL

What is irritating about love is that it is a crime that requires an accomplice.
                                CHARLES BAUDELAIRE

When we want to read of the deeds that are done for love, whither do we turn? To the murder column.

                        GEORGE BERNARD SHAW

The only true love is love at first sight; second sight dispels it.   ISRAEL ZANGWILL

Love is two minutes fifty-two seconds of squishing noises. It shows your mind isn't clicking right.
                                    JOHNNY ROTTEN

Love is the triumph of imagination over intelligence.
H. L. MENCKEN

Love is the word used to label the sexual excitement of the young, the habituation of the middle-aged, and the mutual dependence of the old.
JOHN CIARDI

Boy Meets Girl, So What?   BERTOLT BRECHT

_____ LOVE LETTERS _____

It is well to write love letters. There are certain things for which it is not easy to ask your mistress face to face, like money, for instance.
HENRI DE REGNIER

_____ LOVERS _____

The reason that lovers never weary each other is because they are always talking about themselves.
FRANÇOIS DE LA ROCHEFOUCAULD

OSCAR LEVANT

Total Recoil

OSCAR LEVANT was born in Pittsburgh, Pennsylvania, in 1906, the son of Russian-Jewish immigrants. His parents ran a jewelry store and were music lovers, his father an opera addict, his mother a Tchaikovsky fan.

Levant joked that he tried to run away from home at the age of ten months, and that at the age of ten years, when asked what he wanted to be when he grew up, he replied, "I want to be an orphan." He was an unattractive child with a poor self-image whose high-school classmates awarded him a lemon for being the school's worst dancer (and, typically, he had a pathological aversion to lemons for the rest of his life).

He showed early promise as a pianist, and at sixteen he left home to study music in New York, where he supported himself by giving piano lessons and by playing with dance bands. An appearance in a Broadway musical led to a part in its film version in 1929. He stayed in Hollywood for several years and there met George Gershwin. They became close friends, and Levant virtually abandoned his own career as a composer and became the foremost interpreter of Gershwin's works. He was profoundly shaken by Gershwin's death in 1937.

He worked as a songwriter at MGM in the forties and appeared in several movies, often as himself, i.e., a chain-smoking, wisecracking, tortured genius whose normal facial expression was one of amused disgust.

Although he never got past high school, he was knowledgeable on a variety of subjects and was a regular panelist on *Information Please,* a popular forties radio quiz show.

During the fifties and sixties he appeared sporadically on TV talk shows and stunned viewers with his caustic repartee and frank discussion of his psychiatric problems. He was a manic depressive, an insomniac, and a hypochondriac. He was prey to numerous obsessive rituals: he always buttoned his shirt from the bottom, always stirred his coffee in the same direction four times; when he turned on a water faucet, he tapped it eight times, and when he turned it off, he recited a silent prayer: "Good luck, bad luck, good luck, Romain Gary, Christopher Isherwood and Krisna Menon."

He began taking sleeping pills to control stage fright, and by the end of his life he was a walking pharmacopeia. (He once described Demerol as "better than sex.") A veteran analysand, he was an in-patient in various psychiatric hospitals where he was subjected to a variety of "therapies," including shock treatments. (While confined to the psychiatric ward of a Catholic hospital he complained, "You need a permit from the pope to get two Bufferin here.")

During his career he befriended many of the show business greats of his era—he was a close friend and confidant of George S. Kaufman and Groucho Marx—but those who knew him more casually described him best:

> He seems to me to be one of those truly unquenchable human beings in whom the flame of light burns very brightly, but who, just by virtue of that circumstance, finds its strains and tensions the more agonizing; sometimes unbearably so.
> MALCOLM MUGGERIDGE

> Oscar . . . is full of contempt for himself. And good neurotic that he is, he is willing to share this contempt with the world.
> BEN HECHT

> He has no meanness; and it is doubtful if he ever for a moment considered murder.
> DOROTHY PARKER

Oscar Levant was in constant flight from life, yet he embraced it with a kind of demented joy. He found endless sources of discomfort, annoyance, guilt, and fear, but he was capable of laughing at all of them. He wrote three semiautobiographical books: *A Smattering of Ignorance, The Memoirs of an Amnesiac,* and *The Unimportance of Being Oscar,* which reveal a sensitive, almost tender lunatic who lashed out at everything within his considerable intellectual reach but who always saved the most biting commentary for himself.

His last television appearances were in 1963, on *The Tonight Show,* hosted by Jack Paar. After Levant's death in 1972, Paar closed all his shows with, "Good night, Oscar Levant, wherever you are."

LEVANT ON LEVANT

Under this flabby exterior is an enormous lack of character.

―――――――

I am no more humble than my talents require.

―――――――

I'm a self-made man. Who else would help?

―――――――

I'm a study of a man in chaos in search of frenzy.

―――――――

When I was young I looked like Al Capone, but I lacked his compassion.

―――――――

I never read bad reviews about myself, because my friends invariably tell me about them.

―――――――

I don't drink; I don't like it—it makes me feel good.

―――――――

I was voted Pill of the Year by the Pharmaceutical Society.

There is a thin line between genius and insanity. I have erased this line.

I was once thrown out of a mental hospital for depressing the other patients.

Instant unconsciousness has been my greatest passion for ten years.

Politics? I could have delivered the mental illness vote in a solid bloc.

If you are created by Dostoevsky, like I am, euphoria comes in handy.

The first thing I do in the morning is brush my teeth and sharpen my tongue.

OSCAR LEVANT ANECDOTES

He was able to discourse interminably on the subject of his own greatness, and on one occasion he subjected Aaron Copland to a lengthy diatribe. Unable to stand it anymore, Copland got up to leave. "Why, Aaron, you're becoming an egomaniac. You used to be able to listen to me all night."

Seated at dinner next to an attractive young lady, Levant failed to stifle a yawn. "Am I keeping you up?" she asked. "I wish you were," he answered.

He had three daughters with his non-Jewish second wife. He referred to his family as the *goyim* and exhorted his children to "Finish your martinis before you leave the table."

When introduced to Greta Garbo, Oscar quipped, "Sorry, I didn't catch the name." He later remarked that he had been so overcome by her glamour that all he could do was to stammer the line that ironically has become a prime example of his self-possessed wit.

His first wife subsequently married movie theater tycoon Arthur Loew. At two A.M. on their wedding night, Levant called her and asked, "What's playing at the Loew's State and what time does the feature go on?"

In the late fifties he hosted a local TV show in Los Angeles with his second wife, June, and one night he fell asleep while interviewing a guest. When June tried to nudge him awake, he groused, "Wake me when he's through."

To an obnoxious acquaintance: "I'm going to memorize your name and throw my head away."

After dinner at the White House, Levant turned to his wife and said, "Now I suppose we'll have to have the Trumans over to *our* house."

During a poker game he was told of Judy Garland's latest suicide attempt. "Let's see," he said, dealing a hand, "she's two up on me in suicide attempts, but I'm three up on her in nervous breakdowns. Or is it the other way around?"

QUOTES ON "M"

I believe the best definition of man is the ungrate-
ful biped.   FEODOR MIKHAILOVICH DOSTOEVSKY

Man is a clever animal who behaves like an imbecile.
ALBERT SCHWEITZER

The earth has a skin and that skin has diseases;
one of its diseases is called man.
FRIEDRICH WILHELM NIETZSCHE

Man is a hating rather than a loving animal.
REBECCA WEST

Man is a dog's ideal of what God should be.
HOLBROOK JACKSON

What is a man? A miserable little pile of secrets.
ANDRÉ MALRAUX

Perhaps the only true dignity of man is his capacity to despise himself.   GEORGE SANTAYANA

Man is a puny, slow, awkward, unarmed animal.
JACOB BRONOWSKI

What is man, when you come to think upon him,
but a minutely set, ingenious machine for turning,
with infinite artfulness, the red wine of Shiraz into
urine?   ISAK DINESEN

I love mankind; it's people I can't stand.
CHARLES SCHULTZ

————————————— MANNERS —————————————

Manners are especially the need of the plain. The pretty can get away with anything.
EVELYN WAUGH

To succeed in the world it is not enough to be stupid, you must also be well-mannered.
VOLTAIRE

————————————— MARRIAGE —————————————

Marriage, *n*. The state or condition of a community consisting of a master, a mistress and two slaves, making in all, two.   AMBROSE BIERCE

Marriage is a triumph of habit over hate.
OSCAR LEVANT

He marries best who puts it off until it is too late.
H. L. MENCKEN

I couldn't see tying myself down to a middle-aged woman with four children, even though the woman was my wife and the children were my own.
JOSEPH HELLER

The days just prior to marriage are like a snappy introduction to a tedious book.
WILSON MIZNER

No man, examining his marriage intelligently, can fail to observe that it is compounded, at least in part, of slavery, and that he is the slave.

H. L. MENCKEN

All tragedies are finished by death; all comedies are ended by a marriage.   LORD BYRON

The trouble with wedlock is that there's not enough wed and too much lock.   CHRISTOPHER MORLEY

The chain of wedlock is so heavy that it takes two to carry it—sometimes three.

ALEXANDRE DUMAS *père*

Marriage is like paying an endless visit in your worst clothes.   J. B. PRIESTLEY

When two people are under the influence of the most violent, most insane, most delusive, and most transient of passions, they are required to swear that they will remain in that excited, abnormal and exhausting condition until death do them part.

GEORGE BERNARD SHAW

Marriage is popular because it combines the maximum of temptation with the maximum of opportunity.   GEORGE BERNARD SHAW

A ceremony in which rings are put on the finger of the lady and through the nose of the gentleman.

HERBERT SPENCER

The surest way to be alone is to get married.

GLORIA STEINEM

A friendship recognized by the police.
ROBERT LOUIS STEVENSON

One should always be in love. That is the reason one should never marry. OSCAR WILDE

Marriage is the only adventure open to the cowardly. VOLTAIRE

Marriage makes an end of many short follies—being one long stupidity.
FRIEDRICH WILHELM NIETZSCHE

Courtship to marriage, as a very witty prologue to a very dull play. WILLIAM CONGREVE

The dread of loneliness is greater than the fear of bondage, so we get married. CYRIL CONNOLLY

Marriage: a souvenir of love. HELEN ROWLAND

I got married the second time in the way that, when a murder is committed, crackpots turn up at the police station to confess the crime.
DELMORE SCHWARTZ

Marriage is an arrangement by which two people start by getting the best out of each other and often end by getting the worst.
GERALD BRENAN

Love is an ideal thing, marriage a real thing; a confusion of the real with the ideal never goes unpunished. JOHANN WOLFGANG VON GOETHE

Nothing to me is more distasteful than that entire complacency and satisfaction which beam in the countenances of a newly married couple.

CHARLES LAMB

The most happy marriage I can picture . . . would be the union of a deaf man to a blind woman.

SAMUEL TAYLOR COLERIDGE

Since the law prohibits the keeping of wild animals and I get no enjoyment from pets, I prefer to remain unmarried.
KARL KRAUS

―――――――――――― MARTYRDOM ――――――――――――

It is often pleasant to stone a martyr, no matter how much we admire him.
JOHN BARTH

Martyrdom is the only way in which a man can become famous without ability.

GEORGE BERNARD SHAW

A thing is not necessarily true because a man dies for it.
OSCAR WILDE

Martyrdom covers a multitude of sins.

MARK TWAIN

There is a certain impertinence in allowing oneself to be burned for an opinion.
ANATOLE FRANCE

Great persecutors are recruited among martyrs whose heads haven't been cut off.

E. M. CIORAN

MASTURBATION

Don't knock masturbation—it's sex with someone
I love.   WOODY ALLEN

The good thing about masturbation is that you
don't have to dress up for it.   TRUMAN CAPOTE

MEDICAL PROFESSION

We have not lost faith, but we have transferred it
from God to the medical profession.
                            GEORGE BERNARD SHAW

MEDIOCRITY

Some men are born mediocre, some men achieve
mediocrity, and some men have mediocrity thrust
upon them.   JOSEPH HELLER

Women want mediocre men, and men are working hard to become as mediocre as possible.
                            MARGARET MEAD

MEMORANDUM

A memorandum is written not to inform the reader
but to protect the writer.   DEAN ACHESON

MEN AND WOMEN

The main difference between men and women is
that men are lunatics and women are idiots.
                            REBECCA WEST

Women represent the triumph of matter over mind, just as men represent the triumph of mind over morals.   OSCAR WILDE

MENCKEN'S LAW

Whenever *A* annoys or injures *B* on the pretense of saving or improving *X, A* is a scoundrel.
                    H. L. MENCKEN

METHOD ACTING

Method acting? There are quite a few methods. Mine involves a lot of talent, a glass and some cracked ice.   JOHN BARRYMORE

MIAMI BEACH

Miami Beach is where neon goes to die.
                    LENNY BRUCE

MIDDLE AGES

We owe to the middle ages the two worst inventions of humanity—gunpowder and romantic love.
                    ANDRÉ MAUROIS

MIDDLE CLASS

In the middle classes, where the segregation of the artificially limited family in its little brick box is horribly complete, bad manners, ugly dresses, awkwardness, cowardice, peevishness and all the pretty vices of unsociablity flourish like mushrooms in a cellar.   GEORGE BERNARD SHAW

The middles cleave to euphemisms not just because they're an aid in avoiding facts. They like them also because they assist their social yearnings toward pomposity. This is possible because most euphemisms permit the speaker to multiply syllables, and the middle class confuses sheer numerousness with weight and value.   PAUL FUSSELL

_____ MILITARY INTELLIGENCE _____

Military intelligence is a contradiction in terms.
GROUCHO MARX

_____ MILITARY JUSTICE _____

Military justice is to justice what military music is to music.   GEORGES CLEMENÇEAU

_____ MISSIONARY _____

Missionaries are going to reform the world whether it wants to or not.   OSCAR WILDE

Our noble society for providing the infant Negroes in the West Indies with flannel waistcoats and moral pocket handkerchiefs.
CHARLES DICKENS

Missionaries, my dear! Don't you realize that missionaries are the divinely provided food for destitute and underfed cannibals? Whenever they are on the brink of starvation, Heaven in its infinite mercy sends them a nice plump missionary.
OSCAR WILDE

Make money and the whole nation will conspire
to call you a gentleman.

GEORGE BERNARD SHAW

The chief value of money lies in the fact that one
lives in a world in which it is overestimated.

H. L. MENCKEN

When it is a question of money, everybody is of
the same religion. VOLTAIRE

It is a kind of spiritual snobbery that makes people
think they can be happy without money.

ALBERT CAMUS

Those who have some means think that the most
important thing in the world is love. The poor
know that it is money. GERALD BRENAN

The two most beautiful words in the English language are "check enclosed." DOROTHY PARKER

People will swim through shit if you put a few
bob in it. PETER SELLERS

Virtue has never been as respectable as money.

MARK TWAIN

To be clever enough to get a great deal of money,
one must be stupid enough to want it.

G. K. CHESTERTON

Money cannot buy health, but I'd settle for a diamond-studded wheelchair. DOROTHY PARKER

MONROE, MARILYN

A vacuum with nipples. OTTO PREMINGER

There's a broad with her future behind her.
CONSTANCE BENNETT

She was good at playing abstract confusion in the same way a midget is good at being short.
CLIVE JAMES

MORALITY

Morality is the weakness of the mind.
ARTHUR RIMBAUD

Go into the street and give one a man a lecture on morality and another a shilling, and see which will respect you most. SAMUEL JOHNSON

Bourgeois morality is largely a system of making cheap virtues a cloak for expensive vices.
GEORGE BERNARD SHAW

Morality is the theory that every human act must be either right or wrong, and that 99 percent of them are wrong. H. L. MENCKEN

Morality consists in suspecting other people of not being legally married.
GEORGE BERNARD SHAW

Morality is a disease which progresses in three
stages: virtue—boredom—syphilis. KARL KRAUS

Morality is simply the attitude we adopt toward
people we personally dislike.   OSCAR WILDE

The infliction of cruelty with a good conscience is
a delight to moralists—that is why they invented
hell.   BERTRAND RUSSELL

Moral indignation is jealousy with a halo.
                                    H. G. WELLS

_____ MORNING _____

Getting out of bed in the morning is an act of
false confidence.   JULES FEIFFER

_____ MOTHER _____

Mother is the dead heart of the family, spending
father's earnings on consumer goods to enhance
the environment in which he eats, sleeps, and
watches television.   GERMAINE GREER

_____ MOTHER-IN-LAW _____

I know a mother-in-law who sleeps with her glasses
on, the better to see her son-in-law suffer in her
dreams.   ERNEST COQUELIN

A mother-in-law dies only when another devil is
needed in hell.   FRANÇOIS RABELAIS

If you must choose between living with your
mother-in-law and blowing out your brains, don't
hesitate—blow out hers.   VICTORIEN SARDOU

_____ MURALS IN RESTAURANTS _____

The murals in restaurants are on a par with the
food in museums.   PETER DE VRIES

_____ MUSIC _____

Music is the refuge of souls ulcerated by happiness.
E. M. CIORAN

The chief objection to playing wind instruments is
that it prolongs the life of the player.
GEORGE BERNARD SHAW

Of all noises, I think music is the least disagreeable.
SAMUEL JOHNSON

Musical people always want one to be perfectly
dumb at the very moment when one is longing to
be absolutely deaf.   OSCAR WILDE

Let a short Act of Parliament be passed, placing all
street musicians outside the protection of the law,
so that any citizen may assail them with stones,
sticks, knives, pistols, or bombs without incurring
any penalites.   GEORGE BERNARD SHAW

Assassins!   ARTURO TOSCANINI to his orchestra

GROUCHO MARX

The Dark One

JULIUS HENRY MARX was born in the Yorkville section of Manhattan in 1890 to an unsuccessful Alsatian tailor nicknamed "Frenchie" and an indomitable, archetypal stage mother named Minnie. Groucho was the third of five sons (Leonard, Arthur, Milton, and Herbert later became Chico, Harpo, Gummo, and Zeppo) and was, by his own account, third in his mother's affections. She referred to him as "the dark one."

The origin of his nickname is disputed. It may have come from the practice of wearing a chamois purse around his neck, a "grouch bag," to protect his vaudeville earnings from the hazards of the road, but more likely it was simply an accurate description of his personality.

He began his career at the age of eleven as a boy singer, a member of The Three Nightengales—Groucho, Gummo, and a girl. A series of musical acts (The Four Nightingales, The Six Musical Mascots) barely earned the brothers a living in vaudeville. Groucho worked as a single off and on and was once stranded in Cripple Creek, Colorado, after a disastrous engagement and had to take a job as a wagon driver until Minnie could send him train fare home. Throughout his early career he encountered tough times and tough audiences. One night in Nacogdoces, Texas, he responded to an especially unruly crowd by announcing, "Nacogdoces is full of roaches."

He started wearing a mustache in an early vaudeville act. One night, late for the curtain, he merely drew it on with greasepaint. The audience didn't seem to notice, so he continued the practice for the rest of his vaudeville career and for most of the Marx Brothers movies. It became his trademark along with the crouched walk and the leering, rolling eyes. He grew into his stage persona: he didn't wear a real mustache until he reached middle age.

It wasn't until 1924, when Groucho was thirty-four, that the Marx Brothers finally made it to Broadway in a revue called *I'll Say She Is*. The show was a hit, their career skyrocketed, and the following year they displayed their unique brand of slapstick insanity in another stage hit, *The Cocoanuts,* written by George S. Kaufman and Morrie Ryskind.

The Cocoanuts became their first movie. The Marx Brothers made a dozen more films over the next decade, all of which embodied Groucho's utter disrespect for authority. He played a series of punning, lascivious con men with names like Rufus T. Firefly, Professor Wagstaff, Doctor Hugo Z. Hackenbush, Otis B. Driftwood, Captain Jeffrey T. Spaulding, and J. Cheever Loophole. *A Night in Casablanca* was their last feature film. Groucho said the fun had gone out of moviemaking after the death of Irving Thalberg, the production chief at MGM who had produced *A Night at the Opera* and *A Day at the Races.*

Groucho never graduated from grammar school and regretted his lack of education all his life. He read voraciously to compensate and secretly wanted to be a writer. He wrote three autobiographical books: *Groucho and Me, Memoirs of a Mangy Lover,* and *The Groucho Letters* and surrounded himself with what he considered "intellectuals," mostly young writers, and quietly helped their careers whenever he could.

From 1950 to 1961, he hosted *You Bet Your Life* on television. Ostensibly a quiz show, it was really a platform for his ad-libs. Contestants were chosen for their ability to act as foils for his slashing wit, and the rules were only loosely observed. He made occasional guest appearances on TV shows during the early seventies and, having enjoyed a renaissance among the baby boom generation, he appeared in a one-man show at Carnegie Hall in 1972 at the age of eighty-two.

He grew increasingly frail and senile and died in 1977 at the age of eighty-six, having outlived all of his brothers and most of his friends and show business contemporaries.

Groucho Marx was an optimist disguised as a cynic. He was incapable of having a serious conversation, compulsively making fun of everything and everyone. He was always "on." Chico said that he would "insult a king to make a beggar laugh."

GROUCHO MARX ANECDOTES

After the success of *Cocoanuts* he bought a house in the suburban Long Island community of Great Neck and inquired about joining a restricted swimming club. The manager told him that the club could not accept his application because of its policy against admitting Jews. Groucho thought for a moment and asked, "Well, then how about my son? He's only *half* Jewish. Can he go in the water up to his waist?"

David Steinberg recalls dining with Groucho at the Brown Derby. A priest came up to the table and said, "Mr. Steinberg, I'm a fan." Steinberg immediately said, "Do you know Groucho Marx?"

"Oh, Mr. Marx, I want to thank you for bringing so much joy into the world."

Groucho quickly replied, "I want to thank you for taking so much out."

Groucho was having problems sexually—premature ejaculation. Someone recommended a topical creme guaranteed to prolong erection. When asked later whether it worked, Groucho reported, "I came rubbing the stuff on."

He was invited by Paramount to a screening of *Samson and Delilah* starring Hedy Lamarr and Victor Mature. At the conclusion of the picture one of the studio executives asked Groucho how he liked it. "Well," Groucho replied, "there's just one problem. No picture can hold my interest where the leading man's tits are bigger than the leading lady's."

A drunken fan careened up to him, slapped him on the back, and said, "Why, you old son of a gun, you probably don't remember me," to which Groucho replied, "I never forget a face, but in your case I'll make an exception."

A guest on his *You Bet Your Life* television show was a woman who had given birth to twenty-two children. "I love my husband," the woman explained sheepishly.

"I love my cigar too," Groucho said, "but I take it out once in a while."

QUOTES ON "N"

_____ NATURE _____

Nature is a hanging judge. ANONYMOUS

_____ NECESSITY _____

"Necessity is the mother of invention" is a silly proverb. "Necessity is the mother of futile dodges" is much nearer the truth.

ALFRED NORTH WHITEHEAD

_____ NEW YORK _____

New York: Where everyone mutinies but no one deserts. HARRY HERSHFIELD

Prison towers and modern posters for soap and whiskey. FRANK LLOYD WRIGHT

New York is the only city in the world where you can get deliberately run down on the sidewalk by a pedestrian. RUSSELL BAKER

The city of right angles and tough, damaged people.

PETE HAMILL

This muck heaves and palpitates. It is multidirectional and has a mayor. DONALD BARTHELME

_____ NOBEL PRIZE _____

I can forgive Alfred Nobel for having invented dynamite, but only a fiend in human form could have invented the Nobel Prize.

GEORGE BERNARD SHAW

The amount of noise which anyone can bear un-
disturbed stands in inverse proportion to his mental capacity.   ARTHUR SCHOPENHAUER

_____ NONCONFORMITY _____

Woe to him inside a nonconformist clique who
does not conform with nonconformity.
                                        ERIC HOFFER

QUOTES ON "O"

The trouble with Oakland is that when you get there, there isn't any there there.

GERTRUDE STEIN

The trouble with Oakland is that when you get there, it's there.   HERB CAEN

OBSCENITY

Obscenity is what happens to shock some elderly and ignorant magistrate.   BERTRAND RUSSELL

Obscenity is whatever gives a judge an erection.

ANONYMOUS

OK

I'm not OK, you're not OK, and that's OK.

WILLIAM SLOANE COFFIN

OLD

A man is as old as the woman he feels.

GROUCHO MARX

OPEN MIND

If you leave the smallest corner of your head vacant for a moment, other people's opinions will rush in from all quarters.   GEORGE BERNARD SHAW

Opera, *n*. A play representing life in another world whose inhabitants have no speech but song, no motions but gestures, and no postures but attitudes.
AMBROSE BIERCE

How wonderful opera would be if there were no singers.
GIOACCHINO ROSSINI

The opera . . . is to music what a bawdy house is to a cathedral.
H. L. MENCKEN

People are wrong when they say that the opera isn't what it used to be. It *is* what it used to be. That's what's wrong with it.
NOEL COWARD

_____ OPERA STAR _____

When an opera star sings her head off, she usually improves her appearance.
VICTOR BORGE

_____ OPTIMISM _____

Optimism is the madness of maintaining that everything is right when it is wrong.
VOLTAIRE

Optimism: the noble temptation to see too much in everything.
G. K. CHESTERTON

Optimism, *n*. The doctrine or belief that everything is beautiful, including what is ugly.
AMBROSE BIERCE

Optimism is the content of small men in high places.
F. SCOTT FITZGERALD

The place where optimism flourishes most is the lunatic asylum. HAVELOCK ELLIS

The basis of optimism is sheer terror.

OSCAR WILDE

Optimist, *n*. A proponent of the doctrine that black is white. AMBROSE BIERCE

The optimist thinks that this is the best of all possible worlds, and the pessimist knows it.

J. ROBERT OPPENHEIMER

An optimist is a man who has never had much experience. DON MARQUIS

_____ OTHER PEOPLE _____

Most people are other people. Their thoughts are someone else's opinions, their lives a mimicry, their passions a quotation. OSCAR WILDE

_____ OYSTERS _____

Oyster, *n*. A slimy, gobby shellfish which civilization gives men the hardihood to eat without removing its entrails! The shells are sometimes given to the poor. AMBROSE BIERCE

QUOTES ON "P"

_____ **PALEY, WILLIAM** _____

He looks like a man who has just swallowed an
entire human being.   TRUMAN CAPOTE

_____ **PARANOIA** _____

A paranoid is a man who knows a little of what's
going on.   WILLIAM BURROUGHS

Even paranoids have real enemies.
               DELMORE SCHWARTZ

_____ **PARENTHOOD** _____

There are times when parenthood seems nothing
but feeding the mouth that bites you.
               PETER DE VRIES

There may be some doubt as to who are the best
people to have charge of children, but there can be
no doubt that parents are the worst.
               GEORGE BERNARD SHAW

The only people who seem to have nothing to do
with the education of the children are the parents.
               G. K. CHESTERTON

Some people seem compelled by unkind fate to
parental servitude for life. There is no form of
penal servitude worse than this.
               SAMUEL BUTLER

The Jewish man with parents alive is a fifteen-year-old boy and will remain a fifteen-year-old boy until they die.   PHILIP ROTH

PATIENCE

Patience, *n*. A minor form of despair, disguised as a virtue.   AMBROSE BIERCE

PATRIOTISM

Patriotism is the last refuge of a scoundrel.
                    SAMUEL JOHNSON

In Dr. Johnson's famous dictionary, patriotism is defined as the last resort of a scoundrel. With all due respect to an enlightened but inferior lexicographer, I beg to submit that it is the first.
                    AMBROSE BIERCE

Patriotism is the willingness to kill and be killed for trivial reasons.   BERTRAND RUSSELL

When you hear a man speak of his love for his country, it is a sign that he expects to be paid for it.   H. L. MENCKEN

"My country right or wrong" is like saying, "My mother drunk or sober."   G. K. CHESTERTON

Patriotism is a pernicious, psychopathic form of idiocy.   GEORGE BERNARD SHAW

Patriotism is the virtue of the vicious.
                    OSCAR WILDE

Patriotism is often an arbitrary veneration of real
estate above principles. GEORGE JEAN NATHAN

PEACE

Peace, *n*. In international affairs, a period of cheat-
ing between two periods of fighting.

AMBROSE BIERCE

PEOPLE

It is absurd to divide people into good and bad.
People are either charming or tedious.

OSCAR WILDE

When there are two conflicting versions of the
story, the wise course is to believe the one in
which people appear at their worst.

H. ALLEN SMITH

The devil is an optimist if he thinks he can make
people meaner. KARL KRAUS

People who have no faults are terrible; there is no
way of taking advantage of them.

ANATOLE FRANCE

The world is populated in the main by people
who should not exist. GEORGE BERNARD SHAW

THE PEOPLE

The people are that part of the state that does not
know what it wants.

GEORGE FRIEDRICH WILHELM HEGEL

Once the people begin to reason, all is lost.
VOLTAIRE

The people are to be taken in very small doses.
RALPH WALDO EMERSON

PERFORMANCE ART

Performance art is created by thin young men and usually consists of dancerly women taking their clothes off, putting on masks, and dumping blood on each other while a sound track screeches out machinery noises.
IAN SHOALES

PESSIMISM

My pessimism extends to the point of even suspecting the sincerity of other pessimists.
JEAN ROSTAND

PESSIMIST

Pessimist: one who, when he has the choice of two evils, chooses both.
OSCAR WILDE

A pessimist thinks everybody is as nasty as himself, and hates them for it.
GEORGE BERNARD SHAW

A pessimist is a person who has had to listen to too many optimists.
DON MARQUIS

PHILADELPHIA

Philadelphia: all the filth and corruption of a big city; all the pettiness and insularity of a small town.
HOWARD OGDEN

Philadelphia, a metropolis sometimes known as
the City of Brotherly Love, but more accurately as
the City of Bleak November Afternoons.

S. J. PERELMAN

PHILANTHROPY

Philanthropy is the refuge of rich people who
wish to annoy their fellow creatures.

OSCAR WILDE

Take egotism out, and you would castrate the
benefactors.   RALPH WALDO EMERSON

PHILOSPHERS

All are lunatics, but he who can analyze his delusions is called a philosopher.   AMBROSE BIERCE

If you wish to understand a philosopher, do not
ask what he says, but find out what he wants.

FRIEDRICH WILHELM NIETZSCHE

PHILOSOPHY

Philosophy, *n*. A route of many roads leading
from nowhere to nothing.   AMBROSE BIERCE

Those who lack the courage will always find a
philosophy to justify it.   ALBERT CAMUS

Our quaint metaphysical opinions, in an hour of
anguish, are like playthings by the bedside of a
child deathly sick.   SAMUEL TAYLOR COLERIDGE

Philosophy teaches us to bear with equanimity the
misfortunes of others.   OSCAR WILDE

Philosophy is an unusually ingenious attempt to
think fallaciously.   BERTRAND RUSSELL

I think I think; therefore, I think I am.
                              AMBROSE BIERCE

_____ PHONOGRAPH _____

Phonograph, *n.* an irritating toy that restores life
to dead noises.   AMBROSE BIERCE

_____ PHOTOGRAPHER _____

The photographer is like the cod, which produces
a million eggs in order that one may reach maturity.
                    GEORGE BERNARD SHAW

_____ PLEASURE _____

Pleasure, *n.* The least hateful form of dejection.
                              AMBROSE BIERCE

_____ POETS _____

In the case of many poets, the most important
thing for them to do . . . is to write as little as
possible.   T. S. ELIOT

A poet more than thirty years old is simply an
overgrown child.   H. L. MENCKEN

Poets, like whores, are only hated by each other.
                    WILLIAM WYCHERLEY

I know that poetry is indispensable, but to what I
could not say.   JEAN COCTEAU

> All bad poetry springs from genuine feeling.
>   OSCAR WILDE

I think that one possible definition of our modern
culture is that it is one in which nine-tenths of our
intellectuals can't read any poetry.
                              RANDALL JARRELL

> Poetry is a religion without hope.
>   JEAN COCTEAU

Poetry and consumption are the most flattering of
diseases.   WILLIAM SHENSTONE

> Blank verse, *n.* Unrhymed iambic pentameters—
> the most difficult kind of English verse to write
> acceptably; a kind, therefore, much affected by
> those who cannot acceptably write any kind.
>   AMBROSE BIERCE

Free verse is like free love; it is a contradiction in
terms.   G. K. CHESTERTON

> Politeness . . . is fictitious benevolence.
>   SAMUEL JOHNSON

Politeness, *n.* The most acceptable hypocrisy.
                                   AMBROSE BIERCE

That roguish and cheerful vice, politeness.
FRIEDRICH WILHELM NIETZSCHE

—————————————— POLITICIANS ——————————————

A good politician is quite as unthinkable as an
honest burglar.   H. L. MENCKEN

One has to be a lowbrow, a bit of a murderer, to
be a politician, ready and willing to see people
sacrificed, slaughtered, for the sake of an idea,
whether a good one or a bad one.
HENRY MILLER

Take our politicians: they're a bunch of yo-yos.
The presidency is now a cross between a popularity contest and a high school debate, with an
encyclopedia of cliches the first prize.
SAUL BELLOW

In order to become the master, the politician poses
as the servant.   CHARLES DE GAULLE

The secret of the demagogue is to make himself as
stupid as his audience so that they believe they are
as clever as he.   KARL KRAUS

Anybody that wants the presidency so much that
he'll spend two years organizing and campaigning
for it is not to be trusted with the office.
DAVID BRODER

A politician is a person with whose politics you
don't agree; if you agree with him he is a statesman.
DAVID LLOYD GEORGE

I once said cynically of a politician, "He'll double-cross that bridge when he comes to it."

OSCAR LEVANT

Have you ever seen a candidate talking to a rich person on television? ART BUCHWALD

POLITICS

Politics, *n.* strife of interests masquerading as a contest of principles. AMBROSE BIERCE

Politics is the diversion of trivial men who, when they succeed at it, become important in the eyes of more trivial men. GEORGE JEAN NATHAN

Being in politics is like being a football coach; you have to be smart enough to understand the game, and dumb enough to think it's important.

EUGENE MCCARTHY

The standard of intellect in politics is so low that men of moderate mental capacity have to stoop in order to reach it. HILLAIRE BELLOC

All politics are based on the indifference of the majority. JAMES RESTON

Politics is not the art of the possible. It consists in choosing between the disastrous and the unpalatable. JOHN KENNETH GALBRAITH

It makes no difference who you vote for—the two parties are really one party representing four percent of the people. GORE VIDAL

Nothing is so admirable in politics as a short memory. JOHN KENNETH GALBRAITH

It is dangerous for a national candidate to say things that people might remember.
EUGENE MCCARTHY

You can fool too many of the people too much of the time. JAMES THURBER

_____ THE POOR _____

We who are liberal and progressive know that the poor are our equals in every sense except that of being equal to us. LIONEL TRILLING

The poor don't know that their function in life is to exercise our generosity. JEAN PAUL SARTRE

It is only the poor who are forbidden to beg.
ANATOLE FRANCE

_____ PORNOGRAPY _____

I don't think pornography is very harmful, but it is terribly, terribly boring. NOEL COWARD

My reaction to porno films is as follows: After the first ten minutes, I want to go home and screw. After the first twenty minutes, I never want to screw again as long as I live. ERICA JONG

_____ POSTERITY _____

Posterity is as likely to be wrong as anybody else.
HEYWOOD BROUN

Posterity is just around the corner.
GEORGE S. KAUFMAN

_____ PRAYER _____

Pray, *n*. To ask the laws of the universe be an-
nulled on behalf of a single petitioner confessedly
unworthy.   AMBROSE BIERCE

_____ PREGNANCY _____

If pregnancy were a book they would cut the last
two chapters.   NORA EPHRON

_____ PREJUDICE _____

I am free of all prejudices. I hate everyone equally.
W. C. FIELDS

I don't like principles. I prefer prejudices.
OSCAR WILDE

A great many people think they are thinking when
they are merely rearranging their prejudices.
WILLIAM JAMES

_____ PRESIDENT _____

These presidential ninnies should stick to throwing out baseballs and leave the important matters
to serious people.   GORE VIDAL

When I was a boy I was told that anybody could
become President; I'm beginning to believe it.
CLARENCE DARROW

You can't learn too soon that the most useful
thing about a principle is that it can always be
sacrificed to expediency.
                        W. SOMERSET MAUGHAM

                Principles have no real force except when one is
                well fed.   MARK TWAIN

It is easier to fight for one's principles than to live
up to them.   ALFRED ADLER

                I like persons better than principles and I like
                persons with no principles better than anything
                else in the world.   OSCAR WILDE

PROCRASTINATION

Never put off until tomorrow what you can do
the day after tomorrow.   MARK TWAIN

PROGRESS

                What we call progress is the exchange of one
                nuisance for another nuisance. HAVELOCK ELLIS

All progress is based upon a universal innate desire on the part of every organism to live beyond
its income.   SAMUEL BUTLER

                Progress celebrates Pyrrhic victories over nature
                and makes purses out of human skin.
                                        KARL KRAUS

Progress is the mother of problems.
                              G. K. CHESTERTON

────────────────── PROMISCUITY ──────────────────

A promiscuous person is someone who is getting
more sex than you are.   VICTOR LOWNES

────────────────── PROTESTANTISM ──────────────────

Definition of Protestantism: hemiplegic paralysis
of Christianity—and of reason.
                    FRIEDRICH WILHELM NIETZSCHE

The chief contribution of Protestantism to human
thought is its massive proof that God is a bore.
                              H. L. MENCKEN

────────────────── PSYCHIATRY ──────────────────

Why should I tolerate a perfect stranger at the
bedside of my mind?   VLADIMIR NABOKOV

The relation between psychiatrists and other kinds
of lunatic is more or less the relation of a convex
folly to a concave one.   KARL KRAUS

Psychiatry enables us to correct our faults by confessing our parents' shortcomings.
                              LAURENCE J. PETER

────────────────── PSYCHOANALYSIS ──────────────────

Psychotherapy: the theory that the patient will
probably get well anyhow, and is certainly a damned
ijjit.   H. L. MENCKEN

Psychoanalysis makes quite simple people feel they're
complex.   S. N. BEHRMAN

> Let the credulous and the vulgar continue to be-
> lieve that all mental woes can be cured by a daily
> application of old Greek myths to their private
> parts.   VLADIMIR NABOKOV

Psychoanalysis is confession without absolution.
                                    G. K. CHESTERTON

> Freud is the father of psychoanalysis. It has no
> mother.   GERMAINE GREER

I just want to make one brief statement about
psychoanlysis: "Fuck Dr. Freud."
                                    OSCAR LEVANT

THE PUBLIC

> The public is a ferocious beast: one must either
> chain it up or flee from it.   VOLTAIRE

The public is a fool.   ALEXANDER POPE

PUBLIC OPINION

> Public opinion, in its raw state, gushes out in the
> immemorial form of the mob's fear. It is piped
> into central factories, and there it is flavored and
> colored, and put into cans.   H. L. MENCKEN

One should respect public opinion insofar as is
necessary to avoid starvation and keep out of prison,
but anything that goes beyond this is voluntary
submission to an unnecessary tyranny.
                                    BERTRAND RUSSELL

Punctuality is the virtue of the bored.
                                    EVELYN WAUGH

_____ PUNNING _____

Hanging is too good for a man who makes puns;
he should be drawn and quoted.   FRED ALLEN

_____ PURITANISM _____

The Puritan hated bear-baiting, not because it gave
pain to the bear, but because it gave pleasure to
the spectators.   THOMAS BABINGTON MACAULAY

Puritanism . . . helps us enjoy our misery while we
are inflicting it on others.   MARCEL OPHULS

There is only one honest impulse at the bottom of
Puritanism, and that is the impulse to punish the
man with a superior capacity for happiness.
                                    H. L. MENCKEN

_____ PUBLISHERS _____

As repressed sadists are supposed to become po-
licemen or butchers so those with irrational fear of
life become publishers.   CYRIL CONNOLLY

I could show you all society poisoned by this class
of person—a class unknown to the ancients—who,
not being able to find any honest occupation, be it
manual labor or service, and unluckily knowing
how to read and write, become the brokers of
literature, live on our works, steal our manuscripts,
falsify them, and sell them.   VOLTAIRE

Just a Little Jewish Girl Trying to Be Cute

DOROTHY ROTHSCHILD was born in West End, New Jersey, on August 22, 1893, to a Jewish father and a Scottish-American mother who died in her infancy. Her father remarried, and Dorothy was raised by a stepmother who sent her to a Catholic convent school and later to a private finishing school.

In 1917, following her first literary job as a caption writer for

Vogue, she became a reviewer for *Vanity Fair,* where Robert Benchley was her editor. She was fired on the grounds that her reviews were too tough, and Benchley quit in sympathy. They shared a free-lance office for a time, which prompted her famous crack: "If the office had been any smaller, it would have been adultery."

Her marriage to Edwin Pond Parker II of Hartford lasted only a few years, but she continued to use his name, finding it preferable to her own.

In 1925, she was one of a group of writers who helped Harold Ross found *The New Yorker,* and she became its drama critic in 1927, writing stinging book reviews under the pseudonym of "Constant Reader." Her short stories appeared in the magazine until 1955. She produced light, satirical verse and pessimistic short stories about loneliness, disillusionment, love gone wrong, and suicide. She was never satisfied with her literary efforts—she strove for truth and purity but never felt she had achieved them. About her verse she once said, "I'm always chasing Rimbauds."

Her screenwriting credits include the original version of *A Star Is Born,* and she collaborated on two plays, *Close Harmony* with Elmer Rice and *Ladies of the Corridor* with Arnaud D'Usseau.

In 1933, she married Alan Campbell, an actor-writer eleven years her junior and a homosexual. They went to Hollywood together as screenwriters, were divorced in 1947, and remarried in 1950. When Campbell died in 1963, Mrs. Parker returned to New York to live out her remaining years.

Her reputation as a wit was based more on her conversational bon mots than on her writing, and it grew to the point that many clever remarks were erroneously attributed to her, even though she scrupulously disavowed them. Conversely, two of her most famous lines have been repeatedly misattributed to others: "You can lead a horticulture but you can't make her think" and "Men seldom make passes at girls who wear glasses" (which is frequently misquoted as "Men *never* make passes at girls who wear glasses.")

She was the only regular female member of the Algonquin Round Table, and her cynicism extended to the vicious circle itself: "The Round Table thing was *greatly* overrated. It was full of people looking for a free lunch and asking, 'Did you hear the funny thing I said yesterday?' "

She ridiculed what she considered cultural snobbery: When asked if she had attended the most recent performance of the Philharmonic or the latest museum exhibit, her standard reply was, "I've been too fucking busy and vice versa."

Toward the end of her life she had difficulty writing and missed book review deadlines until she was no longer assigned to write them. But her oral wit remained intact; she still talked brilliantly about her reading material, which remained voluminous and eclectic until her death. But having outlived her fame, she became a bitter, alcoholic recluse. She attempted suicide several times and died in 1967 at the age of seventy-four.

Mrs. Parker's description of herself is emblematic of her attitude toward the rest of the world: "Boy, did I think I was smart. I was just a little Jewish girl trying to be cute."

DOROTHY PARKER ANECDOTES

She often vented her contempt for pretension and self-importance on Clare Boothe Luce, and their encounters produced two famous Parkerisms: When told that Mrs. Luce was always kind to her inferiors, Mrs. Parker asked, "Where does she find them?" On another occasion the two women arrived simultaneously at the door of a nightclub. "Age before beauty," was all Mrs. Luce could muster.

"And pearls before swine," said Mrs. Parker as she glided through the doorway.

Her husband, Alan Campbell, had just died, and as his body was being removed from the house, a female acquaintance asked Dorothy if there was anything she could do. "Get me a new husband," she replied.

"Why, that's the most callous, disgusting remark I've ever heard," the woman said.

Mrs. Parker turned to her and said quietly, "Okay, then run down to the corner and get me a ham and cheese on rye and tell them to hold the mayo."

When a woman told her, "I really can't come to your party, I can't bear fools," Mrs. Parker answered, "That's strange, your mother could."

On being told that President Calvin Coolidge had just died, she remarked, "How could they tell?"

She is credited with saying at a party, "One more drink and I'll be under the host."

On hearing that a British actress who was notorious for her numerous love affairs had broken her leg, Mrs. Parker quipped, "She must have done it sliding down a barrister."

Oscar Levant once asked her if she took sleeping pills, and she replied, "In a big bowl with sugar and cream."

She was confined in an oxygen tent after one of several suicide attempts but was sufficiently in possession of herself to ask, "May I have a flag for my tent?"

She was hospitalized for alcoholism, and her doctor told her that she would be dead in a month if she did not stop drinking. She looked up at him and whispered, "Promises, promises."

QUOTES ON "R"

Radio: the triumph of illiteracy.
JOHN DOS PASSOS

Radio: death in the afternoon and into the night.
ARTHUR MILLER

Radio is a bag of mediocrity where little men with carbon minds wallow in sluice of their own making.
FRED ALLEN

RAT RACE

The trouble with the rat race is that even if you win, you're still a rat. LILY TOMLIN

REAGAN, RONALD

A triumph of the embalmer's art. GORE VIDAL

REFORMERS

All reformers, however strict their social conscience, live in houses just as big as they can pay for.
LOGAN PEARSALL SMITH

RELATIONSHIPS

It is explained that all relationships require a little give and take. This is untrue. Any partnership demands that we give and give and give and at the

last, as we flop into our graves exhausted, we are
told that we didn't give enough.

QUENTIN CRISP

Almost all of our relationships begin and most of
them continue as forms of mutual exploitation, a
mental or physical barter, to be terminated when
one or both parties run out of goods.

W. H. AUDEN

RELATIVES

Relations are simply a tedious pack of people who
haven't got the remotest knowledge of how to live,
nor the smallest instinct about when to die.

OSCAR WILDE

RELIGION

Religion consists in a set of things which the
average man thinks he believes and wishes he was
certain.   MARK TWAIN

All religions are founded on the fear of the many
and the cleverness of the few.   STENDHAL

You never see animals going through the absurd
and often horrible fooleries of magic and religion.
Only man behaves with such gratuitous folly. It is
the price he has to pay for being intelligent but
not, as yet, quite intelligent enough.

ALDOUS HUXLEY

Most religions do not make men better, only warier.

ELIAS CANETTI

The idea of a good society is something you do not need a religion and eternal punishment to buttress; you need a religion if you are terrified of death.   GORE VIDAL

Since the whole affair had become one of religion, the vanquished were of course exterminated.
                                                            VOLTAIRE

Randomness scares people. Religion is a way to explain randomness.   FRAN LEBOWITZ

Religion is the fashionable substitute for belief.
                                                        OSCAR WILDE

We must respect the other fellow's religion, but only in the sense and to the extent that we respect his theory that his wife is beautiful and his children smart.   H. L. MENCKEN

Religion is the venereal disease of mankind.
                                            HENRI DE MONTHERLANT

Religion is the masterpiece of the art of animal training, for it trains people as to how they shall think.   ARTHUR SCHOPENHAUER

Where it is a duty to worship the sun it is pretty sure to be a crime to examine the laws of heat.
                                                        JOHN MORLEY

Truth, in matters of religion, is simply the opinion that has survived.   OSCAR WILDE

Religion is a monumental chapter in the history of human egotism. WILLIAM JAMES

We have just enough religion to make us hate, but not enough to make us love one another.

JONATHAN SWIFT

There is not enough religion in the world to destroy the world's religions.

FRIEDRICH WILHELM NIETZSCHE

The cosmos is a gigantic fly-wheel making 10,000 revolutions a minute. Man is a sick fly taking a dizzy ride on it. Religion is the theory that the wheel was designed and set spinning to give him the ride. H. L. MENCKEN

I'm a born again atheist. GORE VIDAL

_____ RESPECT _____

There was no respect for youth when I was young, and now that I am old, there is no respect for age. I missed it coming and going. J. B. PRIESTLEY

_____ RESPECTABILITY _____

I have always thought respectable people scoundrels, and I look anxiously at my face every morning for signs of my becoming a scoundrel.

BERTRAND RUSSELL

The more things a man is ashamed of, the more respectable he is. GEORGE BERNARD SHAW

Revolution, *n*. In politics, an abrupt change in the form of misgovernment. AMBROSE BIERCE

With the exception of capitalism, there is nothing so revolting as revolution.

GEORGE BERNARD SHAW

Revolution is a trivial shift in the emphasis of suffering. TOM STOPPARD

A revolution is interesting insofar as it avoids like the plague the plague it promised to heal.

DANIEL BERRIGAN

Revolutions have never lightened the burden of tyranny, they have only shifted it to another shoulder. GEORGE BERNARD SHAW

Every revolution evaporates and leaves behind only the slime of a new bureaucracy. FRANZ KAFKA

_____ THE RICH _____

What is the matter with the poor is poverty; what is the matter with the rich is uselessness.

GEORGE BERNARD SHAW

It is the wretchedness of being rich that you have to live with rich people.

LOGAN PEARSALL SMITH

Every man thinks God is on his side. The rich and powerful know he is. JEAN ANOUILH

The rich aren't like us, they pay less taxes.
                              PETER DE VRIES

————————————— RIDICULOUS —————————————

Look for the ridiculous in everything and you find
it.   JULES RENARD

————————————— RIGHT AND WRONG —————————————

Any preoccupation with ideas of what is right and
wrong in conduct shows an arrested intellectual
development.   OSCAR WILDE

————————————— RIVERA, GERALDO —————————————

If Geraldo Rivera is the first journalist in space,
NASA can test the effect of weightlessness on
weightlessness.   ANONYMOUS

————————————— ROCK JOURNALISM —————————————

Most rock journalism is people who can't write
interviewing people who can't talk for people who
can't read.   FRANK ZAPPA

————————————— ROGERS, WILL —————————————

This bosom friend of senators and congressmen
was about as daring as an early Shirley Temple
movie.   JAMES THURBER

————————————— ROMANCE —————————————

When one is in love one always begins by deceiving oneself, and one always ends by deceiving
others. This is what the world calls a romance.
                                OSCAR WILDE

Romance should never begin with sentiment. It should begin with science and end with a settlement.
OSCAR WILDE

Romance, like the rabbit at the dog track, is the elusive, fake, and never attained reward which, for the benefit and amusement of our masters, keeps us running and thinking in safe circles.
BEVERLY JONES

RUSSIA

Ideas in modern Russia are machine-cut blocks coming in solid colors; the nuance is outlawed, the interval walled up, the curve grossly stepped.
VLADIMIR NABOKOV

FRAN LEBOWITZ

Manhattan Malcontent

FRAN LEBOWITZ was born in Morristown, New Jersey, in 1950. In 1968, after attending a series of secondary schools without actually graduating, she moved to New York and took a succession of what she calls "cutesy," jobs—waitress, usher, cab driver—and began writing poetry and book and movie reviews. In 1978, after writing columns in *Mademoiselle* and Andy Warhol's *Interview*, she published *Metropolitan Life*, an anthology of biting, aphoristic commentary whose immediate success made her an overnight celebrity. Her second and most recent book, *Social Studies,* was published in 1981.

JW: *Do you get to Los Angeles often?*
FL: Four, maybe five times a year.
JW: *I gather you're not crazy about it.*
FL: Actually, I like it much better than I used to, probably because I like New York much less. As New York has gotten duller and duller, L.A. seems less awful. I doubt very much that L.A. has *become* less awful, it's just that in contrast to New York it *seems* less awful. You never have to have human contact here; there are very few actual humans to have contact with.

But New York has become so dull. Ed Koch and his Sinclair Lewis boosterism, his "I Love New York" campaign attracted droves of people who don't deserve to live there, people who should live in Atlanta, and it drove out the people who deserve to live there. New York is like Atlanta with very high rents.
JW: *Do you ever try to work while you're out here?*
FL: I hardly try to work anywhere, and by now I have it down to where I cannot work no matter where I am. In my opinion most writers should do less work and not more, and many of them should move here and not work at all. It would be an advantage to the literary world if most writers stopped writing entirely.
JW: *If it's not too personal, how have you been sleeping lately?*
FL: I sleep so poorly. I only sleep in the daytime. It's always been that way, even when I was little. I was sent to bed at 7:30 until I was 10 and thought it was normal. I finally asked my mother why

she made me go to bed so early and she said, "By 7:30 I couldn't listen to you anymore." My mother was in the house all the time and I followed her around; she was the person I talked *at*. That was when I was still asking questions instead of giving answers.

JW: *Do you remember the point when you stopped asking and started answering?*

FL: I had opinions from a young age but mixed them with questions. The only time I ever ask questions now is if I happen to meet a doctor, because I'm a hypochondriac. Other than that I rarely ask questions.

JW: *Tell me about your hypochondria.*

FL: I never worry about things I could actually *get,* like from smoking, but I'll be watching TV and they'll be talking about a disease that only 75-year-old Turkish men get and I'll have every symptom.

JW: *Do you exercise?*

FL: I walk a lot in New York, not for exercise but to get from place to place, and because its the way of having the least contact with human beings. You have to have a death wish to get in a cab. I take the subway when I'm really late, but I prefer to walk because I don't have to put myself at the mercy of that faceless lunatic who drives the subway or the obviously insane man who's driving the taxicab.

JW: *Who doesn't speak English.*

FL: Who doesn't speak any known language at all. Every single cab driver in New York has their name spelled in an alphabet that has an "o" with a slash through it. This is not a language I've ever come in contact with. And now they don't let you smoke in cabs. I'm not going to pay all that money so I cannot smoke.

JW: *Do you watch much television?*

FL: I watch game shows. I was a big fan of "Family Feud." In fact the high point of my career was having an episode of "Family Feud" dedicated to me on the air. The producer called my agent and said they had noticed how often I said I liked the show and they they were going to dedicate a show to me on the air. They did and I watched it and to me it was the Nobel Prize.

JW: *What did you like about the show?*

FL: They had teams of families with five people on each team. The most you could win was $5,000 on the daytime version and $10,000 on the nighttime version. So say you won $10,000; you had to pay your own way to California and you had to pay taxes on the money. I figure it cost the average family about $7,500 to win, and I loved watching them jump up and down before they realized they had only won about $500 apiece. I also liked the answers to the questions. It was like going to a mall without having to leave the house. One of my favorite questions they ever had was, "Name five famous American intellectuals" and the first answer from the winning team was "John Kennedy," a well-known intellectual, and it was on the board! In answer to the question, "Name a famous Rudolph," a guy jumped up and yelled, "Rudolph Hitler!"

JW: *You once said that to you the ultimate activity was autographing your own book. Do you still enjoy it?*

FL: Yes, it's endlessly rewarding. It's a great feeling of accomplishment to have a book in your hand that *you* wrote. And second of all you're *selling* it. Getting money is always a gratifying experience.

JW: *What about celebrity in general—does it bother you to be recognized in public, to have your privacy invaded?*

FL: Writers don't get that famous; the people who have their privacy invaded are mostly movie stars. Writers get exactly the right amount of fame: just enough to get a good table in a restaurant but not enough so that people are constantly interrupting you while you're eating dinner.

JW: *You've been accused of being a snob.*

FL: I'm not a snob in the usual sense. I'm not a *money* snob, I m not a *family* snob, I'm a snob in other ways. I'm an elitist. I do not think everyone is created equal. In fact I know they're not. The Constitution doesn't mean that everyone is as good as everyone else, it means that everyone should have the same *laws* as everyone else. It doesn't mean that everyone's as smart or as cute or as lucky as everyone else. People have distorted the idea of democracy.

JW: *Are you a feminist?*

FL: No. I'm not opposed to most of the goals or beliefs of feminism, but it doesn't interest me. Not that the things feminists say aren't true, they seem to me to be not only true but so obvious that why would you devote your life to worrying about them? It seems to me the sort of thing that a civilized person wouldn't even bother to mention.

JW: *Do you feel that feminism has accomplished anything?*

FL: What has changed? Six people have bigger jobs than they

would have had. Life has not changed for the average woman except for the worse. Now women have to do not only the jobs that they always had to do because men won't do them—I don't care how many episodes of Phil Donahue you watch, men will not do these jobs—they have to do the men's jobs too. The women who fell for this must be in a fury because they used to have boring lives and now they still have boring lives but on top of that they have to work 40 hours a week. It seems to me you were better off when you only had half these problems.

Probably the salient feature of modern life is the idea that everything can be *fixed*. It's a fear of bad luck. I call it "the bad facts." These are the bad facts: Men have much easier lives than women. Men have the advantage. So do white people. So do rich people. So do beautiful people. These are the bad facts. You're born, you take a look at yourself; if you're a black woman instead of a white man your life is ten times harder.

I was recently on the Long Island Expressway going to the airport, surrounded by 11 million people who do this every day. They do this twice a day! And you think to yourself, well, these people obviously feel they're going to live 65,000 years and they figure they might as well spend 30 years sitting in a car. That's how I feel about someone who's an active feminist: you are not going to change anything; if you feel like devoting the little time you have to what I consider a really hopeless cause, you're welcome to do it, but I have no interest in doing it.

JW: *You've said that you don't take drugs.*

FL: I don't take drugs because I don't feel like dying instantaneously. I stopped when I was 19. I never took an hallucinogenic because I never wanted my consciousness expanded one unnecessary iota. I'm sure that being sober all these years accounts for my ill humor.

JW: *You're also on record about romantic love.*

FL: Romantic love is mental illness. But it's a pleasurable one. It's a drug. It distorts reality, and that's the point of it. It would be impossible to fall in love with someone that you really *saw*. The second you meet someone that you're going to fall in love with you deliberately become a moron. You do this in order to fall in love, because it would be impossible to fall in love with any human being if you actually saw them for what they are.

People who get married because they're in love make a ridiculous mistake. It makes much more sense to marry your best friend. You *like* your best friend more than anyone you're ever going to be in love with. You don't choose your best friend because they have a cute nose, but that's all you're doing when you get married; you're saying, "I will spend the rest of my life with you because of your lower lip." It's amazing that all marriages don't end in divorce. If you can stay in love for more than two years, you're *on* something.

QUOTES ON "S"

Saint, *n*. A dead sinner revised and edited.
AMBROSE BIERCE

Saints should always be judged guilty until they are proved innocent. GEORGE ORWELL

SAN FRANCISCO

I'd never set foot in San Francisco. Of all the Sodoms and Gomorrahs in our modern world, it is the worst. It needs another quake, another whiff of fire—and—more than all else—a steady trade wind of grapeshot. That moral penal colony of the world. AMBROSE BIERCE

SANITY

Sanity is a cozy lie. SUSAN SONTAG

SANTA CLAUS

Santa Claus has the right idea: visit people once a year. VICTOR BORGE

SATIRE

Satire is a sort of glass, wherein beholders do generally discover everybody's face but their own. JONATHAN SWIFT

Satire is moral outrage transformed into comic art.
PHILIP ROTH

SALARY

The salary of the chief executive of a large corporation is not a market award for achievement. It is frequently in the nature of a warm personal gesture by the individual to himself.

JOHN KENNETH GALBRAITH

SCANDAL

Scandal is gossip made tedious by morality.

OSCAR WILDE

SCHIZOPHRENIA

Schizophrenia is a successful attempt not to adapt to pseudo-social realities.
R. D. LAING

SCHOOL DAYS

School days, I believe, are the unhappiest in the whole span of human existence. They are full of dull, unintelligible tasks, new and unpleasant ordinances, brutal violations of common sense and common decency.
H. L. MENCKEN

Show me a man who has enjoyed his school days and I'll show you a bully and a bore.

ROBERT MORLEY

SCHOOLMASTER

The average schoolmaster is and always must be essentially an ass, for how can one imagine an intelligent man engaging in so puerile an avocation?
H. L. MENCKEN

Schmucks with Underwoods.   JACK WARNER

_____ SCRIPT _____

There is no such thing as a good script.
JOHN FORD

_____ SELF-CRITICISM _____

Under a forehead roughly comparable to that of
Javanese and Piltdown man are visible a pair of
tiny pig eyes, lit up alternately by greed and
concupiscence.   S. J. PERELMAN

_____ SELF-DENIAL _____

Self-denial is the shining sore on the leprous body
of Christianity.   OSCAR WILDE

Self-denial is not a virtue; it is only the effect of
prudence on rascality.   GEORGE BERNARD SHAW

Self-denial is indulgence of a propensity to forego.
AMBROSE BIERCE

_____ SELF-HATRED _____

He who despises himself esteems himself as a
self-despiser.   FRIEDRICH WILHELM NIETZSCHE

There is luxury in self-reproach. When we blame
ourselves we feel no one else has a right to blame
us.   OSCAR WILDE

SELF-KNOWLEDGE

"Know thyself?" If I knew myself, I'd run away.
JOHANN WOLFGANG VON GOETHE

Know thyself! A maxim as pernicious as it is ugly. Whoever observes himself arrests his own development. A caterpillar who wanted to know itself well would never become a butterfly.

ANDRÉ GIDE

I am the only person in the world I should like to know thoroughly. OSCAR WILDE

SELF-LOVE

To fall in love with yourself is the first secret of happiness. I did so at the age of four and a half. Then if you're not a good mixer you can always fall back on your own company.

ROBERT MORLEY

To love oneself is the beginning of a lifelong romance. OSCAR WILDE

He who is in love with himself has at least this advantage—he won't encounter many rivals.

G. C. LICHTENBERG

If we were not all so excessively interested in ourselves, life would be so uninteresting that none of us would be able to endure it.

ARTHUR SCHOPENHAUER

I find that when I do not think of myself I do not think at all.   JULES RENARD

In an age when the fashion is to be in love with yourself, confessing to being in love with somebody else is an admission of unfaithfulness to one's beloved.   RUSSELL BAKER

—————————— SELF-RESPECT ——————————

Self-respect: the secure feeling that no one, as yet, is suspicious.   H. L. MENCKEN

—————————— SELF-SACRIFICE ——————————

Self-sacrifice enables us to sacrifice other people without blushing.   GEORGE BERNARD SHAW

—————————— SENTIMENTALITY ——————————

Sentimentality is a superstructure covering brutality.
                                    C. G. JUNG

Sentimentality is the emotional promiscuity of those who have no sentiment.   NORMAN MAILER

—————————— SEX ——————————

The pleasure is momentary, the position ridiculous, and the expense damnable.
                                    LORD CHESTERFIELD

Sex: the thing that takes up the least amount of time and causes the most amount of trouble.
                                    JOHN BARRYMORE

Nothing in our culture, not even home computers, is more overrated than the epidermal felicity of two featherless bipeds in desperate congress.
                                        QUENTIN CRISP

Is sex dirty? Only if it's done right.
                                        WOODY ALLEN

In the duel of sex, woman fights from a dreadnaught and man from an open raft.
                                        H. L. MENCKEN

If your sexual fantasies were truly of interest to others, they would no longer be fantasies.
                                        FRAN LEBOWITZ

Men and women, women and men. It will never work.   ERICA JONG

If a man and woman, entering a room together, close the door behind them, the man will come out sadder and the woman wiser.
                                        H. L. MENCKEN

Sexual enlightenment is justified insofar as girls cannot learn too soon how children do not come into the world.   KARL KRAUS

Why should we take advice on sex from the Pope? If he knows anything about it, he shouldn't.
                                        GEORGE BERNARD SHAW

All this fuss about sleeping together. For physical pleasure I'd sooner go to my dentist any day.
                                        EVELYN WAUGH

Sex is the biggest nothing of all time.
ANDY WARHOL

————————— SEXUAL REVOLUTION —————————

The sexual revolution went too far, informationwise. When you find phrases like "suck face" as a euphemism for "kiss" it sort of takes the zing out of intimate personal contact.   IAN SHOALES

————————— SHAW, GEORGE BERNARD —————————

Bernard Shaw is an excellent man; he has not an enemy in the world, and none of his friends like him.   OSCAR WILDE

It is his life work to announce the obvious in terms of the scandalous.   H. L. MENCKEN

He writes his plays for the ages—the ages between five and twelve.   GEORGE JEAN NATHAN

————————— SHIP —————————

Being in a ship is like being in a jail, with the chance of being drowned.   SAMUEL JOHNSON

————————— SILENCE —————————

Silence is the most perfect expression of scorn.
GEORGE BERNARD SHAW

————————— SIN —————————

Sin is geographical.   BERTRAND RUSSELL

The major sin is the sin of being born.
SAMUEL BECKETT

It is dangerous to be sincere unless you are also stupid. GEORGE BERNARD SHAW

A little sincerity is a dangerous thing, and a great deal of it is absolutely fatal. OSCAR WILDE

I don't think you want too much sincerity in society. It would be like an iron girder in a house of cards. W. SOMERSET MAUGHAM

Skepticism is the first step on the road to philosophy. DENIS DIDEROT

I respect faith, but doubt is what gets you an education. WILSON MIZNER

Smoking is, as far as I am concerned, the entire point of being an adult. Many people find smoking objectionable. I myself find many—even more—things objectionable. I do not like aftershave lotion, adults who roller-skate, children who speak French, or anyone who is unduly tan. I do not, however, go around enacting legislation and putting up signs. FRAN LEBOWITZ

It has always been my rule never to smoke when asleep, and never to refrain when awake. MARK TWAIN

I never smoked a cigarette until I was nine. H. L. MENCKEN

There is nothing wrong with sobriety in moderation.   JOHN CIARDI

The function of socialism is to raise suffering to a higher level.   NORMAN MAILER

We should have had socialism already, but for the socialists.   GEORGE BERNARD SHAW

As it will be in the future, it was at the birth of Man.
There are only four things certain since Social
Progress began:—
That the Dog returns to his Vomit and the Sow returns
to her Mire,
And the burnt Fool's bandaged finger goes wabbling
back to the Fire.
RUDYARD KIPLING

Society is a madhouse whose wardens are the officials and police.   AUGUST STRINDBERG

Society attacks early when the individual is helpless.
B. F. SKINNER

Society is always diseased, and the best is most so.
HENRY DAVID THOREAU

SOLITUDE

Solitude would be ideal if you could pick the people to avoid.   KARL KRAUS

SOUTHERN CALIFORNIA

There's nothing wrong with Southern California that a rise in the ocean level wouldn't cure.
                                                    ROSS MACDONALD

Southern California, where the American Dream came too true.   LAWRENCE FERLINGHETTI

SOUTHERNERS

Southerners are probably not more hospitable than New Englanders are; they are simply more willing to remind you of the fact that they are being hospitable.   RAY L. BIRDWHISTELL

SPEED READING

I took a speed reading course and read *War and Peace* in twenty minutes. It involves Russia.
                                                    WOODY ALLEN

When the late President Kennedy was revealed as a speed reader, it took me three hours to read the article about it.   OSCAR LEVANT

SPORTS

The balls used in top class games are generally smaller than those used in others.   PAUL FUSSELL

Serious sport has nothing to do with fair play. It is bound up with hatred, jealousy, boastfulness, disregard of all rules and sadistic pleasure in witnessing violence: in other words it is war minus the shooting.   GEORGE ORWELL

The more violent the body contact of the sports you watch, the lower your class.   PAUL FUSSELL

―――――――――――――― STARLET ――――――――――――――

In Hollywood a starlet is the name for any woman under thirty who is not actively employed in a brothel.   BEN HECHT

―――――――――――――― STATESMAN ――――――――――――――

A statesman is a successful politician who is dead.
THOMAS B. REED

―――――――――――――― STINK ――――――――――――――

Every stink that fights the ventilator thinks it is Don Quixote.   STANISLAW LEC

―――――――――――――― STUDIO HEADS ――――――――――――――

Studio heads have foreheads by dint of electrolysis.
S. J. PERELMAN

―――――――――――――― STUPIDITY ――――――――――――――

Stupidity is an elemental force for which no earthquake is a match.   KARL KRAUS

If you attack stupidity you attack an entrenched interest with friends in government and every walk

of public life, and you will make small progress
against it.   SAMUEL MARCHBANKS

—————————————— SUBURBIA ——————————————

Suburbia is where the developer bulldozes out the
trees, then names the streets after them.
                                        BILL VAUGHN

Slums may well be breeding grounds of crime, but
middle-class suburbs are incubators of apathy and
delirium.   CYRIL CONNOLLY

—————————————— SUCCESS ——————————————

There is an old motto that runs, "If at first you
don't succeed, try, try again." This is nonsense. It
ought to read, "If at first you don't succeed, quit,
quit at once."   STEPHEN LEACOCK

Success is the one unpardonable sin against one's
fellows.   AMBROSE BIERCE

Moderation is a fatal thing. Nothing succeeds like
excess.   OSCAR WILDE

Nothing succeeds like address.   FRAN LEBOWITZ

Nothing succeeds like the appearance of success.
                                CHRISTOPHER LASCH

The desire for success lubricates secret prostitu-
tions in the soul.   NORMAN MAILER

It is not enough to succeed; others must fail.
                                        GORE VIDAL

Success and failure are both difficult to endure. Along with success come drugs, divorce, fornication, bullying, travel, medication, depression, neurosis and suicide. With failure comes failure.

JOSEPH HELLER

Success and failure are equally disastrous.

TENNESSEE WILLIAMS

SUICIDE

Suicide is belated acquiescence in the opinion of one's wife's relatives.   H. L. MENCKEN

There are many who dare not kill themselves for fear of what the neighbors will say.

CYRIL CONNOLLY

If you are of the opinion that the contemplation of suicide is sufficient evidence of a poetic nature, do not forget that actions speak louder than words.

FRAN LEBOWITZ

Dear World: I am leaving because I am bored. I am leaving you with your worries in this sweet cesspool.

GEORGE SANDERS (suicide note, April 25, 1972)

No matter how much a woman loved a man, it would still give her a glow to see him commit suicide for her.   H. L. MENCKEN

I don't think suicide is so terrible. Some rainy winter Sundays when there's a little boredom, you should always carry a gun. Not to shoot yourself, but to know exactly that you're always making a choice.   LINA WERTMULLER

Razors pain you
Rivers are damp;
Acids stain you;
And drugs cause cramp.
Guns aren't lawful;
Nooses give;
Gas smells awful;
You might as well live.
                          DOROTHY PARKER

The thought of suicide is a great consolation: with the help of it one has got through many a bad night.   FRIEDRICH WILHELM NIETZSCHE

SUN

Thank heavens, the sun has gone in, and I don't have to go out and enjoy it.
                          LOGAN PEARSALL SMITH

SUNDAY SCHOOL

A Sunday school is a prison in which children do penance for the evil conscience of their parents.
                          H. L. MENCKEN

SURFNTURF

The surfnturf, as I have always envisioned it, is a tiny, aquatic hereford that has horns and a shell—a beast that moves through the depths slowly, in herds, and can both moo and draw flies under water.   CALVIN TRILLIN

SWEETNESS AND LIGHT

Nobody's interested in sweetness and light.
                              HEDDA HOPPER

SWITZERLAND

Switzerland is simply a large, humpy, solid rock, with a thin skin of grass stretched over it.
                              MARK TWAIN

Switzerland is a curst, selfish, swinish country of brutes, placed in the most romantic region of the world.   LORD BYRON

The only interesting thing that can happen in a Swiss bedroom is suffocation by feather mattress.
                              DALTON TRUMBO

SYMPATHY

I have no need of your God-damned sympathy. I wish only to be entertained by some of your grosser reminiscences.   ALEXANDER WOOLLCOTT

MIKE ROYKO

A Liberal's Conservative and Vice Versa

MIKE ROYKO, the Pulitzer Prize–winning, nationally syndicated columnist for the Chicago *Tribune*, was born in Chicago in 1932. He attended Wright Junior College, the University of Illinois, and Northwestern University. After serving in the U.S. Air Force during the Korean War, he joined the Chicago *Daily News* in 1952 as a reporter and was assigned a weekly government and political column in 1962. His present daily commentary, "Mike Royko," first appeared in the *Daily News* in 1963. He has described his role as follows: "My function is to explain things rather than report them."

JW: *You've written about the deterioration of manners in movie theaters.*

MR: It's the result of television: People are used to talking and they forget that they're not alone when they're in a theater. When I was a kid, I was an usher in a number of theaters and you just told 'em to shut up, and if they didn't shut up, you took 'em out. Today it's anarchy, although I occasionally I go to the movies in a small town in Wisconsin and the kids there are quiet, because for all they know, their uncle may be sitting two rows away. Uncles up there still have crew cuts, half of them are farmers, and they're liable to give the kid a whack in the side of the head. So it's different in smaller communities than it is in a big-city movie theater where if you tell somebody to shut up, he's liable to pull out a knife.

But it isn't just television, it's also the reason why people are carrying guns in their cars and shooting at somebody who cuts them off, why somebody beat up Dan Rather: People are a lot less inhibited when it comes to being uncivilized. It's the age of the jerk.

JW: *In a piece about the "age of the jerk" you wrote that the average politician is a far better man than his average constituent.*

MR: That's true. At the very worst, the politician reflects his constituents. In Chicago we have all these thieves who are alder-men, but they're no worse than the people who elect them. People *do* get the kind of government they deserve.

JW: *Alexander Solzhenitsyn observed that America has no binding ethic. Do you agree?*

MR: The Super Bowl unites us. It's our substitute for war. It's our one unifying element, more so than even the World Series.

JW: *I thought baseball was the national pastime.*

MR: Baseball isn't violent enough, and the games are too long.

JW: *Do you consider yourself a curmudgeon?*

MR: I may have certain tendencies. When I started writing my column, I just wanted to give people a laugh. It's pretty hard to do that with nothing but silly subject matter. If you take on more serious subject matter and try to give them a laugh through that, then I guess it's pretty hard to avoid being curmudgeonly.

There's a problem in writing satire: If you publish it in a sophisticated magazine, you can expect readers to know what you're talking about, but if you write for a newspaper or a bunch of newspapers, readers are easily confused.

JW: *What do you figure is behind this lack of sensitivity to satire?*

MR: There's no laugh track. If we could build in a laugh track, people would know what's funny.

JW: *Are you concerned about the decline in the quality of education in this country?*

MR: No. We went through a period in this country where every-body thought their kid had to have a college education. The result was we got stuck with a whole generation of overeducated dummies. Guys who should be slicing corned beef are mucking around some corporation making dumb decisions. You've gotta have a certain number of people to pump gas and work in the checkout line. If they don't want to learn to read, if they don't want to go beyond the second year of high school, okay, there'll be a job out there for 'em.

JW: *Isn't that an un-American attitude?*

MR: Yeah, but the reality is we can't all be white-collar workers, we can't all be executives, and I don't blame the system. I can go through this newsroom and find kids who came out of affluent backgrounds and had the way paid for 'em, but I can also find reporters who came from families of very modest means and had to hustle to make it. The hustlers will make it, even today.

JW: *Do conservatives think you're liberal, and do liberals think you're conservative?*

MR: More conservatives think I'm liberal than the opposite, but it's close. It's funny what makes somebody a liberal in the conservative mind. I've been against lynching ever since I was a kid, so I guess that makes me a liberal. Civil rights was really the basis for that whole liberal image I had. I started my column in '63, and the one recurring theme in my column was the civil rights movement. That didn't mean that I agreed with every liberal position—I voted for Eisenhower against Adlai Stevenson and I couldn't stand the Kennedys. People who read the column during the sixties thought I was a Commie. My God, I liked Martin Luther King, Jr. That's the basis for the liberal label.

On the other hand, I did a column in which I figured out

what percentage of federal civil service employees are fired in a given year and it's incredible. I can't think of any other work force in America where everybody does their job so well that nobody gets fired. Lawyers get disbarred, doctors get sued for malpractice, but federal bureaucrats are all so good that only one tenth of one tenth of one percent ever lose their jobs. Is that a liberal position? Of course not. The real classic liberals want bigger and better federal government. I believe in political patronage because you can fire a patronage worker.

JW: *You've advocated public hangings for incompetent bureaucrats.*

MR: I've advocated public hangings for a lot of things. Littering, for example. You hear people say, "There's so much mess in the parks." Well, the people who work in the park system don't go around with bushels of litter throwing it around. They don't say, "Okay, guys, here's a hundred pounds of chicken bones, let's throw 'em all over the parks." People are slobs; they won't walk twenty feet to dump their trash in a can. So I advocated the hanging of litterers in the parks. Just leave the bodies up there for a week. Boy, did I hear from people, some who agreed, some who thought I was cruel.

JW: *Which disturbed you more?*

MR (*laughs*): The ones who thought I was cruel. I preferred the ones who agreed, even though they thought I was serious. I've advocated public hangings for boom boxes, people who always veer out to the left before they make a right turn, anybody whose name appears in a gossip column in a favorable way more than three times a year. For a while I was in favor of executing politicians who lose elections. People would think twice about running for office. A lot of people agreed with me on that.

JW: *You've taken on the National Rifle Association.*

MR: I've always defended machine guns on the grounds that I should be able to buy one. I have poor eyesight, and beyond five feet, I couldn't hit anybody with a pistol. But with a machine gun, you just blast away in the direction of the target and you're bound to hit it. Why should I be deprived of the right to defend my home against Commies and fiends?

JW: *Do you jog?*

MR: I hate running. I'll run in a game—I'll run about a tennis court or a handball court, but it makes me nervous when I see someone jogging. Dogs'll try to bite you. I did a column about a guy in Chicago who used to carry a bat when he jogged through the parks. Dogs would try to bite him. He used to carry spray stuff and that wasn't effective, so he finally started carrying a bat. One day he hit this dog who was chasing him and broke the dog's leg. The woman who owned the dog had him arrested, he had *her* arrested, and Louisville Slugger put out the "Fido Model" bat.

QUOTES ON "T"

I can't take a well-tanned person seriously.
CLEVELAND AMORY

He was *audibly* tan.   FRAN LEBOWITZ

TEACHING

Everybody who is incapable of learning has taken
to teaching.   OSCAR WILDE

He who can, does. He who cannot, teaches.
GEORGE BERNARD SHAW

If you can't do, teach. If you can't teach, teach
phys-ed.   ANONYMOUS

TEENAGERS

Like its politicians and its war, society has the
teenagers it deserves.   J. B. PRIESTLEY

TELETHON

The telethon invokes in me more terror than mirth.
The spectacle of all that self-congratulatory yap
masquerading as conscience, of all those chairmen
of the board passing off public relations as altruism is truly sickening.   HARRY STEIN

TELEVISION

Television: chewing gum for the eyes.
FRANK LLOYD WRIGHT

Television is a medium of entertainment which permits millions of people to listen to the same joke at the same time, and yet remain lonesome.

T. S. ELIOT

Television: the bland leading the bland.

ANONYMOUS

Television—a medium. So called because it is neither rare nor well done.   ERNIE KOVACS

Why should people pay good money to go out and see bad films when they can stay at home and see bad television for nothing?

SAMUEL GOLDWYN

Television is now so desperately hungry for material that they're scraping the top of the barrel.

GORE VIDAL

There is an insistent tendency among serious social scientists to think of any institution which features rhymed and singing commercials, intense and lachrymose voices urging highly improbable enjoyment, caricatures of the human esophagus in normal or impaired operation, and which hints implausibly at opportunities for antiseptic seduction as inherently trivial. This is a great mistake. The industrial system is profoundly dependent on commercial television and could not exist in its present form without it.

JOHN KENNETH GALBRAITH

Television is for appearing on—not for looking at.
NOEL COWARD

Television is a device that permits people who haven't anything to do to watch people who can't do anything.
FRED ALLEN

Television is the first truly democratic culture—the first culture available to everybody and entirely governed by what the people want. The most terrifying thing is what the people want.
CLIVE BARNES

My father hated radio and could not wait for television to be invented so he could hate that too.
PETER DE VRIES

Television is an invention that permits you to be entertained in your living room by people you wouldn't have in your home.
DAVID FROST

Television has lifted the manufacture of banality out of the sphere of handicraft and placed it in that of a major industry.
NATHALIE SARRAUTE

I must say I find television very educational. The minute somebody turns it on, I go to the library and read a good book.
GROUCHO MARX

Television is just one more facet of that considerable segment of our society that never had any standard but the soft buck.
RAYMOND CHANDLER

Imitation is the sincerest form of television.
FRED ALLEN

Television is democracy at its ugliest.
PADDY CHAYEFSKY

_____ TEMPTATION _____

Lead me not into temptation; I can find the way
myself.   RITA MAE BROWN

_____ TEXAS _____

If I owned Texas and Hell, I would rent out Texas
and live in Hell.   PHILIP SHERIDAN

_____ THEOLOGIAN _____

I have only a small flickering light to guide me in
the darkness of a thick forest. Up comes a theologian and blows it out.   DENIS DIDEROT

_____ THEOLOGY _____

Theology is the effort to explain the unknowable
in terms of the not worth knowing.
H. L. MENCKEN

_____ THINKING _____

Most people would die sooner than think; in fact,
they do so.   BERTRAND RUSSELL

Thinking is the most unhealthy thing in the world,
and people die of it just as they die of any other
disease.   OSCAR WILDE

Few people think more than two or three times a
year; I have made an international reputation for
myself by thinking once or twice a week.
GEORGE BERNARD SHAW

_____ TIME _____

Time is a storm in which we are all lost.
WILLIAM CARLOS WILLIAMS

So little time, so little to do.   OSCAR LEVANT

_____ TIPPING _____

The man who tips a shilling every time he stops
for petrol is giving away annually the cost of
lubricating his car.   J. PAUL GETTY

_____ TRADITION _____

The longer I live the more keenly I feel that whatever was good enough for our fathers is not good
enough for us.   OSCAR WILDE

_____ TRAVEL _____

People travel for the same reason as they collect
works of art: because the best people do it.
ALDOUS HUXLEY

The most common of all antagonisms arises from
a man's taking a seat beside you on the train, a
seat to which he is completely entitled.
ROBERT BENCHLEY

TRUST

People who have given us their complete confidence believe that they have a right to ours. The inference is false; a gift confers no rights.
FRIEDRICH WILHELM NIETZSCHE

TRUTH

The pure and simple truth is rarely pure and never simple.
OSCAR WILDE

TV BABIES

The first TV babies are now writing with a TV mind that has no attention span at all.
GORE VIDAL

TYRANNY

There are few minds to which tyranny is not delightful.
SAMUEL JOHNSON

QUOTES ON "U"

UGLINESS

It was not until I had attended a few postmortems that I realized that even the ugliest human exteriors may contain the most beautiful viscera, and was able to console myself for the facial drabness of my neighbors in omnibuses by dissecting them in my imagination.

J. B. S. HALDANE

UNIVERSE

My theology, briefly, is that the universe was dictated, but not signed.   CHRISTOPHER MORLEY

It is inconceivable that the whole Universe was merely created for us who live in this third-rate planet of a third-rate sun.

ALFRED LORD TENNYSON

It is impossible to imagine the universe run by a wise, just and omnipotent God, but it is quite easy to imagine it run by a board of gods. If such a board actually exists it operates precisely like the board of a corporation that is losing money.

H. L. MENCKEN

UPPER CLASS

If you are an author and give one of your books to a member of the upper class, you must never expect him to read it.   PAUL FUSSELL

QUOTES ON "V"

Vincent van Gogh's mother painted all of his best things. The famous mailed decapitated ear was a figment of the public relations firm engaged by van Gogh's dealer.   ROY BLOUNT, JR.

VEGETABLES

I have no truck with lettuce, cabbage, and similar chlorophyll. Any dietician will tell you that a running foot of apple strudel contains four times the vitamins of a bushel of beans.

S. J. PERELMAN

Vegetables are interesting but lack a sense of purpose when unaccompanied by a good cut of meat.
FRAN LEBOWITZ

VICE

My only aversion to vice,
Is the price.

VICTOR BUONO

He hasn't a single redeeming vice.
OSCAR WILDE

VIRGINITY

Virginity is the ideal of those who want to deflower.
KARL KRAUS

Virtue is insufficient temptation.
GEORGE BERNARD SHAW

Virtue has never been as respectable as money.
MARK TWAIN

Woman's virtue is man's greatest invention.
CORNELIA OTIS SKINNER

What men call social virtues, good fellowship, is commonly but the virtue of pigs in a litter, which lie close together to keep each other warm.
HENRY DAVID THOREAU

What is virtue but the trades unionism of the married?
GEORGE BERNARD SHAW

———————————— VOTE ————————————

I never vote for anyone. I always vote against.
W. C. FIELDS

He's Gotta Go

MERLE KESSLER was born in 1949, grew up in North Dakota, South Dakota, and Minnesota, and now lives in California with his wife and two daughters. He is a member of Duck's Breath Mystery Theatre, the San Francisco–based comedy group, and is the author of two collections of essays, *I Gotta Go* and *Perfect World*. He is the coauthor, with Dan Coffey, of *The Dr. Science Big*

Book of Science (Simplified). His commentary as the grouchy, fast-talking Ian Shoales is a regular feature on National Public Radio's "All Things Considered."

JW: *What's been bugging you lately?*
MK: Greed, the unbridled greed that's justified in "Lifestyle and Living" columns as being a form of art. Greed has turned into art, and all this talk of Ginnie Maes and Fannie Maes annoys me. "Starter homes." How the hell can you live in a "starter home"? This is like calling your wife your "first wife." It's a very negative way of looking at life.
JW: *What about nuclear disarmament?*
MK: If I were president, I would throw all our nuclear weapons away. That's why I'll never be elected president.
JW: *Ian Shoales has written, "Go ahead and sneer, it's your right." Where exactly does that right come from?*
MK: Ian Shoales's job is to have no enthusiasms—except every once in a while, just to prove he's a human being. It's his job to say no in a world where everyone says yes to every lame idea that comes down the pike.
JW: *Do you consider yourself a curmudgeon?*
MK: No. I consider myself a guy who's trying to make a buck without being stupid.

The funny thing about curmudgeons is that they're mad because life isn't what they wanted it to be. They're expressing a point of view, and even that's rare these days. Someone like Madonna doesn't have a point of view. She's an image, she's High

Concept. There's no moral point of view. If you talk about "moral point of view," people look at you like you're crazy. They don't know what that means. If you bring it up, they look at you like, "What're you, a monk or what?" No, I'm just a normal guy who's trying to make a living in show business without dressing in a clown suit.

JW: *Let me shoot a few subjects at you: contented people.*

MK: There are people who are contented; usually they're aunts and uncles and grandpas. It's kind of a false contentment you see sometimes in places like Marin County. They have this blank look that seems to say, "Since we've taken est . . ." Maybe humans aren't meant to be content. Americans seek Nirvana and inner peace and all that stuff, but I don't think it's in our American genes. If you want to be contented, you should be a dog.

JW: *Communism.*

MK: It's a silly ideology, almost as silly as Mormonism. Most of the tenets of anything are based on really silly premises. Mormons avoided the whole question of Indians and salamanders and gold tablets by creating this intricate and highly successful social structure. Communism avoided the whole question of its viability by killing everybody who wouldn't do things its way.

JW: *Children.*

MK: My wife and I just had a baby, and there's nothing relaxed about them. They're like these little tense things who scream in order to fall asleep. Just like adults, only more direct.

JW: *Any thoughts on the medical profession?*

MK: As the technology becomes more and more sophisticated,

once they're able to discover more and things about the fetus, having a baby will be like shopping. You'll be able to select children's careers before they're born: "Looks like a plumber. Better abort."

JW: *How about lawyers?*

MK: I make fun of lawyers a lot, but actually I've liked every lawyer I've ever met. They're really an unnecessary profession, though. What do they *do*? They don't produce anything. All they do is guide you through the labyrinth of the legal system that they created—and they keep changing it just in case you start to catch on.

It's just like the world of high finance: If you don't understand it, you should stay out of it. I don't understand the law, so I have a lawyer to protect me from it.

JW: *Who protects you from the lawyer?*

MK: Another lawyer.

JW: *How do feel about New York?*

MK: It's overpriced, it's dark, it's insular, it has absolutely no idea what's going on in the rest of the country. The only thing it cares about is what it creates itself, and most of that is an illusion. I think its days as a cultural force are numbered. New York is a horrible place.

JW: *Los Angeles.*

MK: L.A. has the same problem: It pays absolutely no attention to anything except itself.

JW: *Liberals.*

MK: Their hearts are in the right place, I guess. I just saw this movie, *Atomic Cafe*. There's a part about the Rosenbergs—they didn't give you any *information* about the Rosenbergs, just pictures of them with cellos playing on the sound track. It's just cheap sentimentality not connected to anything, and it bothers me. It's like showing pictures of bludgeoned baby harp seals.

JW: *Conversatives*.

MK: Showing pictures of bludgeoned baby harp seals and showing pictures of aborted fetuses are the same trick. Conservatives are mainly greedy assholes, and that's their problem. Not *all* of them, but the climate Reagan has created has brought a lot of these scum out of the woodwork.

JW: *Then you're not a fan of William F. Buckley?*

MK: I think Buckley's a fool who spends too much time caressing dictionaries. Remember when he and Gore Vidal were at the Democratic convention and Vidal called Buckley a crypto-Nazi and Buckley called Vidal a faggot? That's American politics in a nutshell, folks. These are our commentators.

JW: *How about Gore Vidal as a writer?*

MK: He can be funny, but I don't think much of his writing. He's a much better conversationalist than he is a writer. *Myra Breckinridge* wasn't even good pornography.

JW: *He says nobody got it*.

MK: Nobody *got* it? Went right over America's head, did it? I must have missed the rhetorical point of the butt-fucking scene.

JW: *Psychiatry*.

MK: It's a ridiculous profession and it's getting worse. It's becoming almost like palm reading or phrenology. It's been relegated to pop best-sellers and talk shows. The only people that take it seriously are upper-middle-class people who are lonely and can afford to pay someone to listen to them.

JW: *Star Wars*.

MK: Star Wars is simply a waste of money. It's a Hollywood "High Concept," and there's absolutely no way it can work. It proves again that Reagan doesn't have a brain in his head. A defense policy named for a movie? Give me a break. Sometimes I think America likes Reagan, but they're a little disappointed that they couldn't get Jimmy Stewart.

JW: *Tanning*.

MK: I don't understand that stuff at all. You go to the beach and you see people just *lying* there. Read a book! Read a magazine! Go swimming! What are you, a plant?

JW: *The human race*.

MK: I think we'd probably be better off if humans had never existed. Dogs, on the other hand, are perfect creatures.

JW: *How so?*

MK: Unquestioning loyalty, undying love, they're friendly, they can do tricks. Ian Shoales doesn't have a dog, but Merle Kessler does.

JW: *Anything else you'd like to get off your chest?*

MK: Lots of things, but it's getting late and, well, I gotta go.

QUOTES ON "W"

WAR

War is, at first, the hope that one will be better off; next, the expectation that the other fellow will be worse off; then, the satisfaction that he isn't any better off; and, finally, the surprise at everyone's being worse off.   KARL KRAUS

As long as war is looked upon as wicked, it will always have its fascination. When it is looked upon as vulgar, it will cease to be popular.

OSCAR WILDE

War is like love; it always finds a way.

BERTOLT BRECHT

Human war has been the most successful of our cultural traditions.   ROBERT ARDREY

How is the world ruled and how do wars start? Diplomats tell lies to journalists and then believe what they read.   KARL KRAUS

WAR CRIMES

Only the winners decide what were war crimes.

GARY WILLS

WEDDING

The music at a wedding procession always reminds me of the music of soldiers going into battle.   HEINRICH HEINE

Wedding, *n.* A ceremony at which two persons undertake to become one, one undertakes to become nothing and nothing undertakes to become supportable.   AMBROSE BIERCE

_____ WELFARE _____

As far as unwed mothers on welfare are concerned, it seems to me they must be capable of some other form of labor.   AL CAPP

A government that robs Peter to pay Paul can always depend upon the support of Paul.
                        GEORGE BERNARD SHAW

_____ WEST, MAE _____

A plumber's idea of Cleopatra.   W. C. FIELDS

_____ WESTERN CIVILIZATION _____

It would be a good idea.
                        MOHANDAS K. GANDHI

_____ WHITE RACE _____

The white race is the cancer of history. It is the white race and it alone—its ideologies and inventions—which eradicates autonomous civilizations wherever it spreads, which has upset the ecological balance of the planet, which now threatens the very existence of life itself.
                        SUSAN SONTAG

I prefer the wicked rather than the foolish. The
wicked sometimes rest.
ALEXANDRE DUMAS *père*

Wickedness is a myth invented by good people to
account for the curious attractiveness of others.
OSCAR WILDE

Wife: a former sweetheart.   H. L. MENCKEN

The comfortable estate of widowhood is the only
hope that keeps up a wife's spirits.   JOHN GAY

A man likes his wife to be just clever enough to
comprehend his cleverness, and just stupid enough
to admire it.   ISRAEL ZANGWILL

Wife: one who is sorry she did it, but would
undoubtedly do it again.   H. L. MENCKEN

Never feel remorse for what you have thought
about your wife. She has thought much worse
things about you.   JEAN ROSTAND

Men's wives are usually their husbands' mental
inferiors and spiritual superiors; this gives them
double instruments of torture.   DON HEROLD

Woman would be more charming if one could fall
into her arms without falling into her hands.
                              AMBROSE BIERCE

A woman will always sacrifice herself if you give
her the opportunity. It's her favorite form of
self-indulgence.   W. SOMERSET MAUGHAM

The way to fight a woman is with your hat. Grab
it and run.   JOHN BARRYMORE

A woman will flirt with anybody in the world as
long as other people are looking on.
                              OSCAR WILDE

A woman occasionally is quite a serviceable substitute for masturbation. It takes an abundance of
imagination, to be sure.   KARL KRAUS

Brigands demand your money or your life; women
require both.   NICHOLAS MURRAY BUTLER

No woman has ever stepped on Little America—
and we have found it to be the most silent and
peaceful place in the world.   RICHARD E. BYRD

Women are like elephants to me—I like to look at
'em, but I wouldn't want to own one.
                              W. C. FIELDS

Never try to impress a woman, because if you do
she'll expect you to keep up to the standard for the
rest of your life.   W. C. FIELDS

Woman was God's *second* mistake.
                    FRIEDRICH WILHELM NIETZSCHE

Nature has given woman so much power that the
law cannot afford to give her more.
                    SAMUEL JOHNSON

On one issue, at least, men and women agree:
they both distrust women.   H. L. MENCKEN

Women who insist upon having the same options
as men would do well to consider the option of
being the strong, silent type.   FRAN LEBOWITZ

That woman speaks eighteen languages, and she
can't say "No" in any of them.
                    DOROTHY PARKER

The charms of a passing woman are usually in
direct relation to the speed of her passing.
                    MARCEL PROUST

Friendship among women is only a suspension of
hostilities.   ANTOINE DE RIVAROL

When women kiss, it always reminds one of prize-
fighters shaking hands.   H. L. MENCKEN

Women give us solace, but if it were not for women we should never need solace.
DON HEROLD

There is nothing that binds one to a woman like the benefits one confers on her.
W. SOMERSET MAUGHAM

The prostitute is the only honest woman left in America.
TI-GRACE ATKINSON

What passes for woman's intuition is often nothing more than man's transparency.
GEORGE JEAN NATHAN

There's nothing so similar to one poodle dog as another poodle dog, and that goes for women, too.
PABLO PICASSO

A woman without a man is like a fish without a bicycle.
GLORIA STEINEM

The history of woman is the history of the worst form of tyranny the world has ever known: the tyranny of the weak over the strong. It is the only tyranny that lasts.
OSCAR WILDE

Why is the word *tongue* feminine in Greek, Latin, Italian, Spanish, French, and German?
AUSTIN O'MALLEY

To win a woman in the first place one must please her, then undress her, and then somehow get her clothes back on her. Finally, so she will allow you to leave her, you've got to annoy her.

JEAN GIRAUDOUX

The allurement that women hold out to men is precisely the allurement that Cape Hatteras holds out to sailors: they are enormously dangerous and hence enormously fascinating.

H. L. MENCKEN

Whatever women do they must do twice as well as men to be thought half as good. Luckily this is not difficult. CHARLOTTE WHITTON

Most women are not so young as they are painted.

MAX BEERBOHM

He gets on best with women who knows how to get on without them. AMBROSE BIERCE

Women should be obscene and not heard.

GROUCHO MARX

I hate women because they always know where things are. JAMES THURBER

Wicked women bother one. Good women bore one. That is the only difference between them.

OSCAR WILDE

What do women want? SIGMUND FREUD

I do not like work even when someone else does
it.   MARK TWAIN

> Work is of two kinds: first, altering the position of
> matter at or near the earth's surface relatively to
> other matter; second, telling other people to do
> so. The first kind is unpleasant and ill-paid; the
> second is pleasant and highly paid.
>   BERTRAND RUSSELL

Anyone can do any amount of work, provided it
isn't the work he's supposed to be doing at that
moment.   ROBERT BENCHLEY

> By working faithfully eight hours a day, you may
> eventually get to be a boss and work twelve hours
> a day.   ROBERT FROST

Everything considered, work is less boring than
amusing oneself.   CHARLES BAUDELAIRE

_____ WORLD _____

> The world is something that had better not have
> been.   ARTHUR SCHOPENHAUER

The world is a vast temple dedicated to Discord.
                                    VOLTAIRE

> In this world, nothing is certain but death and
> taxes.   BENJAMIN FRANKLIN

We do not have to visit a madhouse to find disordered minds; our planet is the mental institution of the universe.

JOHANN WOLFGANG VON GOETHE

The world is a prison in which solitary confinement is preferable. KARL KRAUS

The whole world is a scab. The point is to pick it constructively. PETER BEARD

In the fight between you and the world, back the world. FRANK ZAPPA

Is not the whole world a vast house of assignation to which the filing system has been lost?

QUENTIN CRISP

The world is a funny paper read backwards—and that way it isn't so funny.

TENNESSEE WILLIAMS

It's a man's world, and you men can have it.
KATHERINE ANNE PORTER

This world is a comedy for those who think and a tragedy for those who feel. HORACE WALPOLE

If the world were a logical place, men would ride side-saddle. RITA MAE BROWN

The world is a spiritual kindergarten where bewildered infants are trying to spell God with the wrong blocks. EDWIN ARLINGTON ROBINSON

Maybe this world is another planet's hell.
ALDOUS HUXLEY

God created the world, but it is the Devil who keeps it going.
TRISTAN BERNARD

When you leave New York, you are astonished at how clean the rest of the world is. Clean is not enough.
FRAN LEBOWITZ

WRITERS

One reason the human race has such a low opinion of itself is that it gets so much of its wisdom from writers.
WILFRID SHEED

The dubious privilege of a freelance writer is he's given the freedom to starve anywhere.
S. J. PERELMAN

There are no dull subjects. There are only dull writers.
H. L. MENCKEN

WRITING

All writing is garbage. People who come out of nowhere to try to put into words any part of what goes on in their minds are pigs.
ANTONIN ARTAUD

If you can't annoy somebody, there's little point in writing.
KINGSLEY AMIS

If I didn't have writing, I'd be running down the street hurling grenades in people's faces.
PAUL FUSSELL

QUOTES ON "Y"

Youth is a wonderful thing. What a crime to waste it on children.　　GEORGE BERNARD SHAW

Youth is a period of missed opportunities.
CYRIL CONNOLLY

It is one of the capital tragedies of youth—and youth is the time of tragedy—that the young are thrown mainly with adults they do not quite respect.
H. L. MENCKEN

The young always have the same problem—how to rebel and conform at the same time. They have now solved this by defying their parents and copying one another.　　QUENTIN CRISP

What is youth except a man or a woman before it is ready or fit to be seen?　　EVELYN WAUGH

The denunciation of the young is a necessary part of the hygiene of older people, and greatly assists the circulation of the blood.
LOGAN PEARSALL SMITH

THE YULETIDE CURMUDGEON

I am sorry to have to introduce the subject of Christmas. It is an indecent subject; a cruel, gluttonous subject; a drunken, disorderly subject; a wasteful, disastrous subject; a wicked, cadging, lying, filthy, blasphemous and demoralizing subject. Christmas is forced on a reluctant and disgusted nation by the shopkeepers and the press: on its own merits it would wither and shrivel in the fiery breath of universal hatred; and anyone who looked back to it would be turned into a pillar of greasy sausages.

GEORGE BERNARD SHAW

I believed in Christmas until I was eight years old. I had saved up some money carrying ice in Philadelphia, and I was going to buy my mother a copper-bottomed clothes boiler for Christmas. I kept the money hidden in a brown crock in the coal bin. My father found the crock. He did exactly what I would have done in his place. He stole the money. And ever since then I've remembered nobody on Christmas, and I want nobody to remember me either.

W. C. FIELDS

Christmas is a holiday that persecutes the lonely, the frayed and the rejected.   JIMMY CANNON

Something in me resists the calendar expectation
of happiness.   J. B. PRIESTLEY

Next to a circus there ain't nothing that packs up
and tears out any quicker than the Christmas spirit.
                                        KIN HUBBARD

Bah, Humbug!   EBENEZER SCROOGE

ROY BLOUNT, JR.

This Man Is Not a Murderer

THE *Sports Illustrated* contributor and author of collections of essays and verse, including *Not Exactly What I Had in Mind, One Fell Soup,* and *What Men Don't Tell Women,* isn't in a terrific mood.

JW: *Before we begin, would you please sign this release?*
RB: Why do you have to have this?

JW: *My publisher requested I have all the interview subjects sign it.*

RB (*reads and rereads release, then reads aloud*): ". . . releases liability for any activity including [*raises voice*] invasion of the rights of privacy, libel and copyright infringement." I'm signing away my rights. I can't do that. [*winces and laughs derisively*].

JW: *If that's the only objectionable part of it, just cross it out and initial it.*

RB: Okay. [*Signs and initials the release.*] Why would anybody expect anybody to sign something like this? Nobody wants to sign away their right to sue for libel. I mean, what if you said in the book that I was a murderer?

JW: *It's the product of an overzealous lawyer, I guess.*

RB: Yeah, the world is full of overzealous lawyers.

JW: *Do you consider yourself at all curmudgeonly or misanthropic?*

RB (*laughs derisively*): No. Who would do that?

JW: *Well, I grant you that it's uncurmudgeonly to characterize oneself as a curmudgeon, but I'm basing it on some of the things you've written.*

RB: Like what?

JW: *Like what you wrote about Christmas, for example.*

RB: What'd I say about Christmas?

JW: *You said that if a kid is smart enough to understand the concept of Santa Claus by Thanksgiving, he'll see through it by December fifteenth.*

RB: I never set out to be a curmudgeon.

JW: *Okay, let's try something a little closer to home. You've written lots of articles for* Sports Illustrated. *What do you think of John McEnroe?*

RB: I think he's a bully and I don't like bullies. He bullies old, fat men. He's a spoiled kid. Lately maybe he's a burned-out kid. He reminds me of Bobby Fisher, who seemed to me a mixture of baby and tyrant. I think that's an unattractive mixture. He's a petulant, callow bully. But he's a very good tennis player. On the other hand, sports do tend to be dominated by ineffectual, bureaucratic amateurs who don't really know what they're doing. I would be sympathetic to anybody who screams at NCAA officials.

JW: *In trying to place you in some sort of curmudgeonly "tradition," I find similarities between your verse and Dorothy Parker's.*

RB: I like her verse. It seems to me that it's a kind of anti-Puritanism that was more attractive to me when I was a kid in a Methodist household than it is now. I still like a lot of those lines, but it seems to me sort of mannered now. I still relish a number of her lines, but Mencken really holds up because Mencken had a better time. Mencken liked a lot of things like beer and loose women, and he liked to have a good time.

When I was in high school, I was reading Mencken and I quoted his definition of a Puritan to my mother: "A Puritan is a person who lives in the fear that someone, somewhere, may be having a good time." My mother liked it because she had a sense of humor, but she said, "You know, we're pretty much Puritans ourselves." I was shocked because I'd never faced up to it conceptually that way.

JW: *You've written that you don't like the woods because "there's no sin there."*

RB: Yeah, I believe in having a sense of sin, a sense of right and wrong. I've never quite understood all the pejorative associations with the word *judgmental*. Obviously you can abuse judgmentalism and you can browbeat people with it, but I think it's wrong *not* to be judgmental. If somebody does something wrong, you have to say it's wrong.

Mark Twain said that the trouble with a lot of Americans was that Puritanism was so solidly established here that you were either Puritan or anti-Puritan and there was no other tradition to hook into, whereas in England you could be a Cavalier or something. There's no real Cavalier tradition in America.

JW: *A lot of writers complain about the fact that the market for books is shrinking and it's becoming more and more difficult to get publishers to promote their books.*

RB: Every author pisses and moans about his publisher. It's a commercial proposition. It costs an enormous amount of money to advertise books. I'm tired of listening to authors gripe about their publishers—I've done enough griping and enough listening to get kind of bored with it all. It's the same story over and over: all the things that are wrong with publishing. There *are* a lot of things wrong with publishing, but on the other hand, I remember when I was a kid growing up in Atlanta what a narrow selection of books were available. Now you can get any kind of book in the world.

JW: *I'd hoped you'd have something nasty to say about publishers.*

RB: The reason I stopped complaining about publishers is that it seems to me that if they were better at marketing, if they were certain about the kind of books they wanted, it would be bad for the writer. I mean, you get frustrated with publishers because they don't seem to know how to sell books. It all seems to be a mystery to them, until a book starts selling, and then they advertise it. You wonder who's in charge here, who's selling the book? But if it ceased to be a mystery, it might well become too mechanical. This way you can still slip through the cracks.

Look, if you can make a living being a writer, it's hard to complain. I was down in a little town in Texas one time writing a story about coon hunts, and I was talking to these guys who were telling me what a wonderful job I had writing for *Sports Illustrated*. And I said, naa, you have to take all these planes and you have to stand in line with your bags and run around the country and it's tiring and you have to stay up late to write the story. One of them said, "I bet it beats runnin' tree saws eight hours a day."